Published by Card and Craft, Inc.

Card and Craft Inc. offers strategic, spiritual, technical and educational support to those who live, work and play in a conscious way.

Tarot Tour Guide

Tarot Tour Guide

TAROT, THE FOUR ELEMENTS,
AND YOUR SPIRITUAL JOURNEY

Christiana Gaudet

Card and Craft, Inc.

Palm City, Florida

The scanning, uploading and distribution of this book via the Internet or via any other means without the permission of the publisher is illegal and punishable by law. Please purchase only authorized editions and do not participate in or encourage the electronic piracy of copyrighted materials. Your support of the author's rights is appreciated.

This is a work of nonfiction. Names used within this work are either used with the permission of the individual, or are names used to protect the identity of those who chose not to reveal their names. No warranty is implied or given about the use of tarot.

TAROT TOUR GUIDE:
TAROT, THE FOUR ELEMENTS, AND YOUR SPIRITUAL JOURNEY
ALL RIGHTS RESERVED
Copyright © Card and Craft Inc, 2019

Cover art by Steven Bright
Edited by Mary K. Wilson, Second Edition Edits by Mary Ellen Collins
Second Edition Interior Formatting by Jana Cole and John Gaudet
ISBN# 978-1-7328797-0-6
Electronic Publication Date: May 2019
Print Publication Date: May 2019

This book may not be reproduced or used in whole or in part by any means existing without written permission from the publisher, Card and Craft, Inc, 1025 SW Martin Downs Blvd Ste 203, Palm City, FL, 34990-2868

For more information please visit the author's website
www.christianagaudet.com

Table of Contents

Second Edition Author Preface xv

Introduction xvii
    Important Words .... *xvii*
    What's in This Book .... *xx*

The Spiritual Journey of Tarot 1
    The Spiritual Journey *2*
    Your Tarot Journal *4*
    Clues for the Beginner- Using Your Tarot Journal *5*
    Your Magickal Journey *5*
    Your Tarot Altar *7*
    Meditation for Awareness of the Spiritual Journey *8*
    The Fool's Journey *10*

The Major Arcana 12
    Greater Secrets *12*
    Card 0 The Fool *13*
    Card 1 The Magician *13*
    Card 2 The High Priestess *14*
    Card 3 The Empress *14*
    Card 4 The Emperor *15*
    Card 5 The Hierophant *15*
    Card 6 The Lovers *16*
    Card 7 The Chariot *16*
    Card 8 Strength *17*
    Card 9 The Hermit *17*
    Card 10 The Wheel of Fortune *18*

Card 11 Justice	19
Card 12 The Hanged Man	19
Card 13 Death	20
Card 14 Temperance	20
Card 15 The Devil	21
Card 16 The Tower	21
Card 17 The Star	21
Card 18 The Moon	22
Card 19 The Sun	22
Card 20 Judgment	23
Card 21 The World	23
Major Arcana Exercises	*24*
Identifying with the Fool	24
Key Words	24
Meditation	25
Exercise for the Advanced Student: Best and Worst	*25*
The Minor Arcana	**26**
Lesser Secrets	*26*
Wands	*28*
Ace	28
Two	29
Three	29
Four	29
Five	30
Six	30
Seven	31
Eight	31
Nine	32
Ten	32
Cups	*32*
Ace	32
Two	33
Three	33
Four	33
Five	34

Six	34
Seven	35
Eight	35
Nine	35
Ten	35

Swords 36
    Ace 36
    Two 36
    Three 37
    Four 37
    Five 37
    Six 38
    Seven 38
    Eight 38
    Nine 39
    Ten 39

Pentacles 39
    Ace 40
    Two 40
    Three 40
    Four 40
    Five 41
    Six 41
    Seven 41
    Eight 42
    Nine 42
    Ten 42

Pip Card Exercises 43
    Four Elements Reading 43
    Storytelling 43
    Runs 43

Exercise for the Advanced Student-Four Elements 43

The Court of the Minor Arcana 45

Meet the Court 49
    Page of Wands 49
    Knight of Wands 49
    Queen of Wands 50
    King of Wands 50
    Page of Cups 51
    Knight of Cups 51

  Queen of Cups 51
  King of Cups 52
  Page of Swords 52
  Knight of Swords 53
  Queen of Swords 53
  King of Swords 53
  Page of Pentacles 53
  Knight of Pentacles 54
  Queen of Pentacles 54
  King of Pentacles 54
  Correspondences of the Court 55

Court Card Exercises 57
  Key Words 57
  Significator 57
  People in Your Life 57
  What to Do? 57
  Numbers Exercise 58

Exercise for the Advanced Student- Expand the Role of Tarot in Your Life 58

Perspectives on Tarot 59
  Four Methods of Tarot Reading 59
  Intuitive Exercise 60
  Exercise for the Advanced Student- Interpretive Reading 60
  Five Ways to See Tarot 61
  Tarot Tool Exercise 63
  Holistic Tarot 63
  Body: The Material World 64
  Mind: The Emotional World 66
  Spirit: The Spiritual World 68
  Body, Mind and Spirit Exercises 69

Reading Tarot 71
  Reversals 72
  Intuitive Reading 72
  Spreads, Questions and Dialogues 73
  Tarot Spreads 74
  Asking Questions in a Reading 76
  Tarot Dialogues 78
  Create your Own Spreads 78
  Tarot Spreads 79

Celtic Cross 79
Seven Sisters Spread 81
Future Vision Spread 81
The Lamplighter Spread 83
Mapping the Spiritual Path Spread 84
Relationship Spread 85

Exercise for the Advanced Student-Spreads *86*

The Four Elements: An Elemental Journey 87

Compass Rose Spread for Elemental Balance 93
Restoring Elemental Balance 95
Four Elements Meditation 96
Summoning the Elements 101
Call to the Quarters 102
Dismissal to the Quarters 103

The Element of Air-Thinking, Learning, Communication, Integrity 105

Invocation of the Air 106
Swords Air Exercise 106
Major Arcana Air Exercise 107
Clues for the Beginner -Air: The Study of Tarot 107
Tarot, Meditation and the Search for Clarity 107
Meditation Exercise 108
Reading for Yourself and Others 108
Exercise: What is a Tarot Reading? 110
Good News, Bad News 111
Tarot, Decisions and Attitudes 115
Sample Reading: Decision Making 118
Tarot Ethics 119
Ethics Exercise 120
Advanced Exercise: Referrals 120
Spotting Truth and Untruth in a Reading 120
Stories from the Suit of Swords 121
Magickal Dedication for your Tarot Journey 122

The Element of Earth- Grounding, Healing, Home, and Abundance 124

Invocation of the Earth 125
Pentacles Earth Exercise 126
Major Arcana Earth Exercise 127

  Clues for the Beginner- Earth: Taking Care of Your Tarot Cards 127
  Plan your Career with Tarot 128
  Finding Your Calling 128
  Career Cards Exercise 131
  Exercise for the Advanced Student- Real Life Career 131
  Tarot Magick to Find Your Calling 131
  Mapping the Path 132
  A Sample Reading using the Mapping the Path Questions 133
  A Sample Career Reading 136
  Divination and Magick for Getting a Job 139
  Career Shifting Spread 141
  Tarot and the Physical Body 141
  Tarot and Attitudes about Money 143
  Stories from the Suit of Pentacles 144
  Tarot Magick for Abundance and Wellness 144

The Element of Water- Love, Sensitivity, Emotion and the Healing Heart. 146

  Invocation of Water 147
  Cups Water Exercise 148
  Major Arcana Water Exercise 148
  Clues for the Beginner- A Two-Card Relationship Spread 149
  Tarot, Self Esteem and Relationships 149
  Exercise for the Advanced Student: Court Card Relationships 151
  Tarot Fellowship and Group Dynamics 151
  Group Exercises 152
  Storytelling 152
  Circle Definitions 153
  Tarot Charades 153
  Round Robin Readings 153
  Introductions 153
  On Your Mind 154
  Predicting and Finding Romance with Tarot 154
  Couples Readings 156
  Sample Reading-Still Single 156
  Sample Reading: Single Again 160
  Tarot as a Tool for Heart-to-Heart Communication 165
  Tarot and the Intuitive Process 167
  Tarot and the End of a Relationship 169
  Stories from the Suit of Cups 171
  Tarot Magick for Love and Healing 171

The Element of Fire- Passion, Creativity, Vitality and Spirituality. 173
    Invocation of Fire 175
    Wands Fire Exercise 176
    Major Arcana Fire Exercise 176
    Clues for the Beginner- Having Fun 176
    Tarot and the Creative Process 177
    The Tower 179
    The Sexual Tarot 179
    Tarot and Divination 181
    Tarot as a Tool for Psychic Development 183
    Tarot and Dreams 184
    Tarot and Spirit Communication 186
    Tarot as a Tool for Creative Visualization 187
    Tarot as a Map for the Spiritual Path 190
    Stories from the Suit of Wands 194
    Tarot Magick to Ignite the Fire Within 195

Continuing the Journey 198

Bibliography and Recommended Reading 199

Index of Figures and Tables 201

About the Author 202

Second Edition Author Preface

When I first began writing the book that became *Tarot Tour Guide*, I had some specific goals in mind. At the time, there were books offering tarot interpretations, and specialty tarot books about tarot magick and tarot for creativity. There were very few books that described an inclusive tarot practice. My idea was that within tarot are lessons for life, growth, and healing, and that tarot-based magick, introspection, and divination could be a meaningful daily spiritual practice. I wanted to share that concept, along with practical ways of accomplishing it. Yet, there was more.

As much as I wanted to share the spiritual journey of tarot, I'm also a practical diviner. So often I see a disconnect between the way we value tarot as a spiritual tool and the we way we value tarot as a fortune-telling tool. The net result of that can be deeply spiritual people who are mediocre tarot readers. The goal of *Tarot Tour Guide* was to present tarot as a spiritual journey and, at the same time, share practical and proven tarot reading techniques developed from my decades-long tarot career.

As I re-read the book in preparation for creating the second edition, I felt that the book had achieved that goal, but only to a point. What stood in the way of my complete satisfaction was that I was, at times, an imprecise writer. Also, I hadn't yet found my tarot voice, nor had I completely mastered the art of quantifying the mystical processes of tarot reading in a way that really made sense. Most importantly, I realized as I read over what I had written so passionately a decade ago that since then, I've grown not only as a writer, but also as a tarotist.

Tarot Tour Guide

Part of that growth comes from social media and the ability to connect with peers from around the world. Part of that growth is that a relationship with tarot is never a stagnant thing.

I'm happy to report that there was nothing I had published in 2012 that I disagreed with upon reading it in 2018. There were a few places I felt I hadn't been clear or thorough. There were also some statements that now seemed dated. When I felt the need, I inserted some thoughts clearly labeled as "Second Edition Author Update".

I've also made some gentle changes to the text in several places, either to correct a typo, expand on a thought, or to improve style or clarity. In creating a second edition of *Tarot Tour Guide*, my goal is to present my original material in a way that is easier to understand and embrace, and to make this book available to the public again.

Each of us develops a unique personal relationship with tarot. Whether you are a beginner, an aficionado, or a professional, it is my hope that this book will help you explore new ways to connect with and learn from tarot, and new ways to allow the cards to speak to you in a reading.

Blessings,

Christiana Gaudet
August 2018
Palm City, Florida

Introduction

When I write about tarot as a tour guide, I'm working from a number of levels.

This book is a tour guide for new tarot students as they begin their tarot journey.

For more experienced readers, I offer new perspectives and ideas, especially the idea that tarot guides us through the spiritual journey of life.

I have long held the belief that tarot is more than a simple fortune-telling device. I want people who read this book to broaden their understanding of tarot as a tool for spiritual growth and to view their tarot study as a spiritual journey.

A metaphysical understanding of the four elements has been a cornerstone of my spiritual journey. Viewing tarot from an elemental perspective makes it easy to learn and use the cards. Viewing life from an elemental perspective gives us the ability to maintain equilibrium on a constantly shifting planet.

In this book, I present the four elements as a way of understanding tarot, and as a way of understanding life.

Important Words

As in any field, the world of tarot has specific words that may be new to you. One of the words you will encounter in this book is *magick*. Many metaphysical practitioners spell magick with a 'k' to separate it from stage magic. In this book, you will learn ways to use tarot cards to attract and manifest your desires. We call this tarot magick.

Second Edition Author Note:
Over the past year I've become aware that many practitioners of magic/magick find the addition of the letter 'k' smarmy and cheesy,

or at least unnecessary. Even knowing this, I would still probably use it because I really do like to have a word different from what we use to describe mundane legerdemain. I did, however, want to acknowledge the ire of those who find this practice unappealing.

* * *

Another word you will see is *querent*. This is an old-fashioned tarot word. It refers to the person who is receiving the tarot reading. Other words used to mean the same thing are questioner, sitter and client.

The word *significator* refers to a tarot card, or position in a tarot spread, that represents a specific person.

Second Edition Author Note:

I wrote my first two books prior to becoming a blogger. Something that the practice of keeping multiple blogs has taught me is that it is often wise to take more time, and more words, to explain things. I think my earlier writing suffered from too much of an economy of words, although no one has ever accused me of speaking too few words!

As I read over my explanation of the word significator, I realized how much more I needed to say here, especially given that this word has virtually no meaning outside of tarot.

The word significator means a card that signifies a specific person.

In early tarot tradition, the significator was a card chosen by the reader from amongst the sixteen Court cards at the beginning of the reading to represent the querent. The significator was intentionally chosen, rather than drawn at random. The reader chose the significator based on the age, gender and appearance of the querent.

The significator would be placed on the table prior to beginning the divination. Energetically, this may be a way to connect the reading to the querent. There may be readers who still work with a significator in this way, although I don't personally know any.

In some traditional methods of reading, the significator is used to determine which cards will supply the reading. For example, in the Opening of the Key method, the significator is chosen and then placed back into the deck. After shuffling, the deck is broken into four piles. The pile in which the significator lands is the pile that will provide the reading.

In many modern tarot reading techniques, the significator is simply a position in a tarot spread. Whatever card falls into that position will signify who the querent is at that moment. This can be a great way of getting a handle on the current energies of the person you are reading for, whether that be a client or yourself.

Today, most tarotists also have a card they refer to as their significator. This is the card that they use to represent themselves; the card with which they always identify. Sometimes it is a Court card, but sometimes not. It may be a Major Arcana card, or a card from the numbered Minor Arcana.

Many tarotists will also have a significator for each of their close friends and family members. When they read for themselves and those particular cards appear, the reader will see how their friends and family members are operating in his or her life.

* * *

In this book, you will learn to *invoke* energies or to perform invocations. An invocation is a process, usually using spoken words, that calls on a particular spirit or energy to bring specific aid. Invocations are like prayers and are used as part of magick.

You will also see the word *divination*. Divination, or the verb "to divine," is to use metaphysical means to seek answers that are not necessarily knowable by mundane means. Tarot is a tool of divination.

Second Edition Author Note:
There is one more word I want to add here, not necessarily because I use it often in this book, but because it is an essential word in the world of tarot and is often misunderstood. The word is *oracle*.

Typically, we tarotists use the word oracle to describe card decks used for divination that do not follow a tarot structure. "Is that angel deck a tarot or an oracle?" is a question you may hear from someone wondering about the structure of a card deck.

This common usage of the word oracle creates a bit of misunderstanding because it is a limited usage when compared to what the word can mean. Truly, an oracle can be any tool of divination, any person who uses such a tool, the message that is revealed in a reading, and even the place in which the reading is performed!

As a diviner, it's good to have this more complete understanding of what this word means, especially if you plan on studying older primary source material. At the same time, it is important to know that, typically, when someone is referring to an oracle, they mean a deck that is used for divination but is not tarot.

* * *

What's in This Book

In this book, you will find descriptions of the seventy-eight tarot cards, as well as tarot spreads. You will find discussions about tarot, and many ways you can use your tarot deck.

Some of what you will find will be traditional tarot information. Some of the information is completely original, gleaned from nearly two decades of professional tarot reading.

With this information, you will be able to learn about the cards, and ways of reading them. You will be able to understand many ways of incorporating tarot as a useful tool in every aspect of your life.

You will also find many tarot exercises that will help you explore tarot hands-on. These exercises may involve pulling cards at random or choosing cards cognitively. The exercises may require you to meditate on a card or to write about a card.

Some exercises and informational sections are specifically for tarot beginners. I've labeled these "Clues for the Beginner," although advanced readers may enjoy them, too.

A few exercises are more complex. I've labeled these "Exercises for the Advanced Student."

I've designed some of the exercises to teach about the four elements, or other spiritual concepts, as well as about the cards.

You will also find guided meditations, and instructions for using tarot for magick and manifestation.

The first chapter of this book discusses the concept of the spiritual journey, and tarot as an important tool on that journey. You will be asked to begin keeping a tarot journal.

Chapters Two, Three and Four of this book will teach a little bit about each of the seventy-eight tarot cards. If you are already familiar with tarot, think of it as a refresher course, or an opportunity to get a new perspective on the cards. Then use your tarot journal to reflect on the cards and enjoy the exercises in each chapter.

If you are new to tarot, take the time to think about each of the cards. You do not need to commit them to memory yet. Simply read the passages, look at your cards, and see if the descriptions and interpretations make sense to you. Then use your tarot journal to do the exercises and enjoy the beginning of your tarot journey.

Chapter Five will introduce you to different ways of seeing and understanding tarot. Chapter Six will show you ways of reading tarot and introduce you to some tarot spreads. Chapter Seven will take you on an in-depth journey into the four elements, and help you understand how to use elemental thinking in tarot interpretation, magick, and to promote personal balance and wellness.

The final four chapters are each dedicated to one of the four elements. Each chapter will show you ways of using tarot to honor that element in your life. You will learn that there is no aspect of life that tarot cannot touch. Tarot can assist you in every possible circumstance you will ever encounter. Tarot truly is a tour guide on the exciting adventure of life.

CHAPTER ONE

The Spiritual Journey of Tarot

Whether you are just beginning your tarot journey, or have been on that journey for years, tarot has a way of staying fresh. There is always something new to learn, a new perspective to consider, or new insights to be revealed.

Tarot is the name given to a deck of cards, but tarot is so much more than simply a deck of cards.

Second Edition Author Note:
It's interesting that many of us speak of tarot as "more than a deck of cards" Historically, tarot began as a game, so in its original sense, tarot is exactly a deck of cards, no more, no less. Now, we see the characters of tarot as telling the story of an epic adventure which is an archetypal journey and an allegory for life. We also see tarot as a specific art form, rendered repeatedly by different artists and in different media.

Of course, this concept of tarot being more that seventy-eight pieces of cardboard also speaks to its value as a book of magickal symbols and spiritual wisdom, as well as its ability to be in our hands a tool for divination and magick.

***

Most tarot decks are comprised of seventy-eight cards, divided into two sections. The Major Arcana, or "Greater Secrets," contains twenty-two cards, numbered zero through twenty-one. Card zero is the Fool. In recent years, tarotists have started referring to the Major Arcana as "The Fool's Journey."

Second Edition Author Note:

This term, "The Fool's Journey", also known as "The Path of the Fool", was first coined by tarot author Eden Gray in the epilogue of her book, *A Complete Guide to Tarot*. This book was published in 1970 and it was my very first tarot book!

❋ ❋ ❋

The structure of the Minor Arcana is like a deck of playing cards. It consists of four suits, ace through ten, with a court of four characters in each suit. In each suit we can see a journey, or a story, just as we do in the Major Arcana.

Many people see tarot only as a tool for divination or fortune telling. Tarot is in fact a very potent divination tool. But if we limit tarot to just divination, we are doing it, and ourselves, a disservice.

Tarot is a guidebook for life. Each card offers a key to unlock spiritual mysteries. As we study tarot, we learn about life and about ourselves. Tarot is a tool of magick, meditation and spiritual discovery.

When we learn to divine with tarot, we develop a powerful connection with our Higher Self, and our Higher Power.

When we understand the versatility of tarot, we enlist tarot as a tour guide on life's journey.

The Spiritual Journey

The term "Spiritual Journey" is a catchphrase that describes any sort of growth and development. You might find this term associated with substance abuse recovery, hallucinogenic drug use, meditation, the creative process, or Christian devotion.

What does it mean?

French philosopher and Jesuit priest Pierre Teilhard de Chardin said that we are not human beings having a spiritual experience. We are spiritual beings having a human experience. Perhaps, then, the spiritual journey is what brings us closer to the knowledge of our true spiritual self. The spiritual journey is our perception of our human experiences as lessons that help us grow and heal along the way.

The lifetime experience and accomplishments of a person cannot be the finite total of who that person is. Life's journey takes us beyond this lifetime. Whether we believe in reincarnation, a rewarding afterlife, or integration into a greater spiritual whole, the concept of a spiritual journey suggests the concept of a spirit that will survive our physical death, and that began before our birth.

The idea of a personal spiritual journey suggests that we live with intent. Every traveler has a destination. The spiritual journey means that we have a spiritual destination. We acknowledge specific goals for personal growth that we wish to fulfill during our lifetime. Sometimes it seems clear that Higher Power has goals for our spiritual growth that we ourselves did not choose.

The spiritual journey of the individual is intensely personal and unique, but no one functions independently of other people. Our spiritual path intertwines with the path of others in infinite ways. When we live life as a purposeful journey of the spirit, we have deep insight into the spiritual nature of our relationships.

Along the journey, we find tools that inspire and guide us. Tarot is such a tool. As a book of spiritual wisdom, tarot gives us a foundation to develop a positive personal philosophy and worldview. As a tool of divination, tarot allows us to communicate with our higher consciousness, and with the spirit world around us. As a set of magickal tools, tarot works to manifest healing and helps us to achieve our highest potential. As a tool of psychic development, tarot helps us to tap into our intuitive skills. As an allegory of the human experience, tarot gives us the framework to understand and celebrate our own existence.

The word *journey* and the word *journal* share a common root word from the French. That root word translates as *daily*. That journey is related to daily suggests that we must be conscious of our spiritual journey every day. We find spiritual meaning in mundane tasks and personal growth in our day-to-day lives.

Many indigenous cultures and modern Earth-based traditions recognize the sacred nature of the mundane and create ritual and myth around the cultivation and preparation of food, and other daily tasks. In our busy modern world, we often forget to seek the sacred in common, every-day things.

The word journal also relates to the word daily, since a journal keeps a daily record. The connection between journal and journey reminds us to document our journey in our journal.

Your Tarot Journal

Most tarot teachers suggest their students keep a tarot notebook, or tarot journal. It can be a simple composition book or a fancy and beautiful blank book. If you already have a tarot journal, take this moment to rededicate it to your study and appreciation of tarot. If you don't have one yet, take the time now to find one.

Second Edition Author Note:

If you prefer working with a tablet or computer, or even with your phone, you can just as easily keep your journal as a digital file. There are even journaling and study apps that you can adapt to your tarot study.

* * *

Use your journal to record your thoughts and ideas about the cards. You can write about the readings and exercises you do, and your own personal musings. This will help you develop a personal understanding of the cards, and of how they speak to you. It will help you find clarity and insight about the most important mystery of all, your own spiritual journey. Your journal will help you discover the secrets of tarot, the secrets of the universe, and the secrets within yourself.

Clues for the Beginner- Using Your Tarot Journal

Set up your journal so that you have one page for each card. Write key words and phrases for each card on its page. As you learn new key words, add them to your list.

In another part of your journal, record your readings, and written exercises.

Many readers like to pull one card a day, at random, usually at the same time each day. If you record the card in your journal, you can go back the next day and write about how that card manifested during the day. Many people call this the COTD, or Card of the Day. When you draw a COTD, meditate with the card you have chosen. How does the image make you feel? Look up interpretations for the card and record the ones that make sense to you. This will help you memorize meanings for each card. More importantly, it will help you decide what each card means to you.

Your Magickal Journey

We are all magickal beings, whether we see it or understand it. A human being is more than the physical body, and even more than personality and memories. Every human being, and every living thing, possesses energy. That energy can be described as a life force, chi energy, or a vibration. We can channel and direct that energy as a force for protection, for healing, and for manifestation. The practice of working with that energy is magick.

Tarot functions as a magickal tool, whether or not we intentionally use it that way. Each card carries a specific energy and draws that energy unto itself. When we use tarot for magick, we find it is a potent ally on our journey.

Aleister Crowley defined magick as "the science and art of causing change to occur in conformity with will". We understand that the change is caused by mystical means rather than mundane actions.

Nearly every religion has some provision for magick, although religious belief is not required to make magick work. Some Christian sects perform faith healing. Most monotheistic religions use prayers of petition. Magick is a cornerstone of many Pagan religions.

There are specific ethics generally associated with magick. Most simply and generally, never use magick to hurt anyone or to manipulate anyone's behavior, actions, or feelings. Use magick to bring healing, whether on a spiritual, emotional, or physical level.

You can use tarot magick to attract something you desire. You can use tarot magick to remove from your life something that no longer serves you.

Divination itself is a magickal practice. Performing divination as part of a sacred rite, or at a holy time, strengthens the connection to the spirit world and deepens the insight of the reading.

Healing is also a magickal practice. Energy work such as Reiki might be considered a form of magick. That Reiki is offered as part of complementary medicine in hospitals throughout the world is a testament to its efficacy.

You can use tarot to send healing to folks in need or to heal yourself. Simply choose a card that represents healing to you, such as the Star, or the Sun, or the World. Or, choose a card that represents the subject once they have received their healing. For instance, you might use the Empress, or the Queen of Wands, to represent a healthy adult woman.

Breathe the energy of the card in and direct your healing intentions to the subject. In your mind's eye, visualize the subject healed. Hold that image in your mind. Connect that image in your mind with the tarot image you hold. Then, carry the image with you, or place it in a sacred place, such as on your altar. You might even want to give the subject a copy of the image.

That is but one small example of how we can use tarot in healing magick.

Self-reflection is one of the best uses of tarot, and even that has a magickal component. The Wiccan Charge of the Goddess says that "if that which you seek you do not find within yourself, you will never find it without." When we can achieve clarity through divination, personal transformation is the obvious next step.

Another aspect of magick is invocation. In ritual work and prayer, tarot cards can be used to invoke elemental energies, deities, angels, saints or loved ones in spirit.

Second Edition Author Note:
Over the past year I have become increasingly impressed with the power that the practice of invocation brings to a tarot reading. I now actively invoke Spirit prior to every tarot reading as a part of preparing for the reading and creating sacred space.

* * *

A simple way to invoke with tarot is to choose a card that represents the energy or entity you are invoking. For instance, The High Priestess could represent the Virgin Mary. The Hermit could represent St. Francis. The four Aces could be used to invoke the four elements. The Moon could represent the Goddess Diana. Use your imagination!

Magick is our helpful companion along the spiritual journey, and tarot is our magickal toolbox.

Your Tarot Altar

Many homes have within them a sacred space to honor a Higher Power or one's ancestors. In some cultures, it is a shrine. In other cultures, it is simply a photograph on the wall or a statue on the mantelpiece.

A table or shelf that holds sacred objects and magickal tools is often called an altar. The altar can be a place to meditate or perform divination or magick. The altar always holds sacred space. This means that no matter what mundane activities happen in your home, the altar is always attuned to a higher energy.

A tarot altar is a wonderful place to meditate with tarot cards, do readings, study tarot or do tarot magick. Even if you already have an altar or shrine in your home, it is nice to have an additional tarot altar.

Your tarot altar is a sacred space set aside to honor your tarot practice. It doesn't mean that you can't read, practice or study tarot anywhere you want. It is simply a way of making space in your life for tarot by making space in your home for tarot. Because the altar will hold the energy of your intentions, it will help bring the knowledge and power of tarot to you. That power will aid in your study, your understanding, your magick and your readings.

If you live in a place where you cannot have a standing altar, try an "altar in a box," and just set it up when you are going to use it.

You may choose to have a special deck of cards just for your altar, and for tarot magick. You may choose to store your reading deck, when not in use, on your altar. You may also have candles, crystals, incense, flowers, statuary, or anything else on your altar that feels right.

Meditation for Awareness of the Spiritual Journey

Meditation is another aspect of tarot practice. We use meditation to help us become more intuitive and to foster inner awareness. Later in this book, you will learn that tarot is a tool of meditation and see how meditation enhances tarot understanding. When we meditate, we are open to communication from our higher selves, our spirit guides, our ancestors and our Higher Power.

This meditation is an easy way to become more aware of your own path as a spiritual being.

Read this meditation once, and then read it aloud into a recorder. Use the recording to guide you through this meditation. Or, have a friend lead you through it.

Create a quiet and sacred space for yourself, perhaps using candles, incense and soft music.

Begin by sitting or lying comfortably and breathing deeply. Start your recording now.

As you breathe out, allow your mundane worries and concerns to leave you. As you breathe in, be aware of your breath as the vehicle that transports you to the meditative state.

Begin your meditation by repeating this affirmation:

My earthly life is a journey of my soul. Each day carries me further. Each challenge has a purpose. I walk in innocence and trust my Higher Power. I walk with purpose and trust my inner knowledge. I look now within myself to see the larger picture. I seek the symbols and ideas that give me guidance.

Take a moment and look within. Are there any immediate symbols or messages that come to you?

Now visualize a landscape of rolling hills. Each one of these hills is a lifetime over which you must journey.

Now zoom in on the hill that represents your current lifetime. Place yourself on that hill and look around. Now that you are closer you can see that your hill contains smaller hills and valleys, streams, rivers and oceans. It may contain cities and forests, animals and people.

Look around and see if you recognize the people and places around you. Where and when on this lifetime's journey are you visiting? Do you recognize things from your past, or your present? Perhaps you have a glimpse into your possible future?

Now look down at your feet. Since the journey is long, it is important to know what will carry you. Are you wearing shoes? Are your feet comfortable?

Perhaps you have a vehicle to help you on your journey. Look around for a bicycle, or a car, or perhaps a boat or even a hot air balloon. What are the vehicles that help you on your journey?

As you travel along, look to see if you have any guides or guardians assisting you. If so, ask them if they have any information to give you.

Now look for any signs along the way. You may see road maps, street signs, or symbols that will help you understand your journey.

When you are ready to end your meditation, look around you and think of the things that you have seen, and what you will want to remember.

Return your breathing to normal and feel yourself connected to the ground beneath you.

Spend a moment reflecting on your meditation, and what it has shown you about your spiritual journey. Write or draw the thoughts or symbols, even the ones you don't currently understand.

Before you leave your sacred space, pull a tarot card at random to give insight about the meditation and help you understand the symbols and signs that you received.

The Fool's Journey

Many tarot beginners, and even some more advanced readers, make the mistake of learning the cards only as individual symbols with meanings. Spiritual tarot seekers, and the best tarot readers, understand that the tarot itself tells a story. In fact, it tells the story of a spiritual journey!

Medieval Europe gave birth to tarot. It also gave birth to another spiritual teaching tool: the morality play. In those times, theatre, as the Greeks and Romans had enjoyed it, was out of favor with the Christian church. A new form of theatre developed, designed to give people spiritual and moral guidance. Many of these morality plays, as they were called, focused on a character that represented all people. This character had a name like Everyman or Mankind.

In each play, the lead character had to confront other characters, such as Temptation, Wealth, Good Deeds, and Humility. The plays were designed to illustrate the spiritual challenges that we each must face and to point the way to the correct choices.

The design of tarot is, in many ways, like the morality plays. But in tarot, the lead character is not called Everyman, or Mankind. In tarot, the lead character is called The Fool.

The Fool is the only card in the tarot that is not numbered. That is because he has no specific place in the deck. Rather, he travels from card to card, experiencing the challenges, lessons and rewards of each card. The Fool travels through the tarot, just as we travel through life. The Fool represents each one of us. The rest of the cards represent the lessons, experiences, and people we encounter.

Although the cards have a specific numerical order, we do not always experience the events and lessons of each card in numerical order. That is why the mechanism of the cards is so important. As a book of spiritual wisdom read from beginning to end, tarot teaches some important lessons. Because the cards can be shuffled and drawn at random, the lessons are as infinite as the possibilities offered by life itself.

We learn the lessons of the tarot each time we read for ourselves and each time we read for someone else. We even learn from the cards while we are learning about the cards.

I hope you will discover, as I have, that tarot can be a vital and versatile tool and teacher on your spiritual journey.

CHAPTER TWO

The Major Arcana

The Major Arcana is the term given to the twenty-two trump cards of the tarot. These are often more ornately illustrated and bear more symbolism than the rest of the cards. Some tarot decks are "Majors Only" and contain just these twenty-two cards. It is quite possible to perform profound and accurate readings with a Majors Only deck, or with the Major Arcana from any deck.

Greater Secrets

The term "Major Arcana" means "Greater Secrets." Each card holds spiritual wisdom, just as each card holds prophetic meaning. Each card represents the important lessons, characters, themes and experiences we encounter in life. Each card has metaphysical attributes, including numerological and elemental associations.

What follows is a brief discussion of some of the traditional images, lessons and divinatory meanings of each of the Major Arcana cards.

The tarot contains universal themes, or *archetypes*. Archetypes are characters, themes and experiences with which we are all familiar. These include the epic journey, the hero's journey, the rise from innocence into experience, the divine couple, the wise old man, the innocent child, and so forth. We see these themes and characters in literature and myth because they reflect the human experience. We can see these archetypes within each of the Major Arcana cards.

As you look through the cards and think about their meanings, see if you recognize these familiar themes. What characters from fiction or history do you see portrayed in the tarot? How do the Major Arcana images reflect the themes and experiences in your own life?

Card 0 The Fool

The Fool is often pictured at a crossroads, or about to walk off a cliff. His countenance is merry. He may carry a white flower to symbolize his innocence. A small dog often accompanies him. The dog may be playing with him, following him, or biting his leg, as if to keep him from taking the wrong path. The Fool carries a pouch. We cannot see within the pouch, but traditionally we believe that the pouch contains the four tools of magick that become the icons for the four suits of the Minor Arcana.

The Fool teaches us to enjoy our path, even if we do not know where we are going. We learn to trust our intuition, and to honor our inner child. Through the Fool we acknowledge that life is a journey, but it does not need to be solemn or laborious.

In a reading, the Fool can indicate decisions, or travel. He may suggest a carefree attitude or a need to embrace the inner child. He may describe a person who is fun and child-like. He may tell you that you have tools at your disposal of which you are not aware. The Fool may encourage you to take a leap of faith.

When reversed, there may be bad decisions or immature behavior. You may be afraid to take a risk or to honor your inner child.

Card 1 The Magician

The Magician is often pictured with the four tools of magick in front of him. One hand points toward the sky, the other points to earth. This indicates the ancient magickal principle "as above, so below," and describes the Magician's ability to channel energy from heaven to Earth and back again. The Magician is in eternal control of his power and his tools.

From the Magician we learn to identify and use our own tools. We learn to take control of our own circumstances, and to use the energy around us to manifest our own will.

The Magician is 'the trickster.' He carries the 'coyote' energy of Native American lore. He possesses the skill to create illusion.

Yet the Magician is also the card of the scholar or the student, and can indicate study, attendance at school or learning new things. The Magician tells us that we have the skills, tools and abilities that we need, and encourages us to develop them. This card speaks of the open mind, and new beginnings.

The reversed Magician may suggest a closed mind, or that we are questioning our tools, skills or abilities. There may be an issue regarding schooling or the acquisition of knowledge. We may not be prepared for the cunning nature of an adversary.

Card 2 The High Priestess

The High Priestess is usually shown sitting between two pillars. She serenely holds a book of wisdom. She wears symbols of balance and spirituality from many cultures.

The High Priestess teaches us to look inward, to seek our own spiritual perfection. From her we learn to find the source of wisdom in greater teachings, but to also find the source of wisdom within ourselves.

In a reading, the High Priestess can represent balance, wisdom, and perfection. She also represents virginity, serenity, and intuition. This is the card of the perfectionist. It can advise meditation and spiritual retreat. It may tell you that you are being too hard on yourself. It may represent a woman who is held in high esteem.

In reversal, the High Priestess may suggest guilty thoughts or actions, or suspicion of inappropriate activities.

Card 3 The Empress

The Empress is often pictured as a pregnant woman. Even if we cannot see her pregnancy, we assume she is in the process of giving life. She is surrounded by the abundance and fertility of nature.

The Empress is the archetypal mother. From her we learn to welcome abundance and fertility and to share it freely. We learn to nurture, to create, and to honor the rhythms and cycles of nature.

The Empress often appears in a reading to represent one's mother, motherhood issues and issues of pregnancy and fertility. She can also represent creativity, abundance, nurturance, and caring for others. This card asks the question: "To what are you ready to give birth?"

The reversed Empress may suggest mothering issues or fertility issues. Selfishness may also be indicated. You may have an issue with your own mother. You may be feeling impoverished, or uninspired.

Card 4 The Emperor

The Emperor sits with a commanding and stern countenance. He is often surrounded by symbols of authority.

The Emperor teaches us leadership and responsibility. As the ruler of the land, he must make fair and wise decisions. He must be consistent and stable in his demeanor. He teaches us to rule our own lives in the same manner.

Although the Emperor is seated, in many depictions we can see that his feet are armored. As a politician, or government leader, he can declare war.

The Emperor may represent a father or male authority figure. He may also indicate issues of governance or business. He may caution or describe an attitude of stability, responsibility or adherence to routine. He may indicate a political environment, or the need for strategy.

The reversed Emperor may be either overbearing or irresponsible. Instability is indicated when this card appears reversed.

Card 5 The Hierophant

The Hierophant is generally pictured as a religious authority. Often, he is the Pope or a bishop. In some modern decks he is shown as a shaman.

The Hierophant helps us to encounter authority. He teaches us to seek authority and to develop and use our own authority. He teaches us to know the rules before we play the game. He may teach us to question authority and to use authority wisely.

In a reading the Hierophant may suggest meetings with authority figures, such as doctors or lawyers. Since the Hierophant speaks of religious rituals and traditions, this is also a card of marriage. The Hierophant represents the learning and teaching of doctrine. Adherence to tradition can be indicated.

In reversal, this card can indicate thinking outside the box, or finding different solutions. It may suggest that you do not have the authority to carry out your plans, or that you are resisting the authority of others.

Card 6 The Lovers

The Lovers is the first Major Arcana card that shows two people of equal stature, usually a male and female. There is also often an angel present, and the couple is sometimes embracing. Sometimes it is a depiction of Adam and Eve. Sometimes the man looks at the woman, while the woman looks at the angel.

The Lovers teaches the lesson of good choices and discernment. Like the mythical Adam and Eve on which this card is based, we have free will. We are responsible for our choices. It is the choices we make that determine our success or failure in love and in life.

In a reading, the Lovers may refer to a love relationship, or to affairs of the heart. It may also speak to decisions that must be made, or to issues of self-esteem and personal security. It may suggest the need to integrate different aspects into a greater whole, or to create balance between opposites.

The Lovers reversed may suggest a lack of self-esteem, a lack of balance and integration, or an inadvisable love relationship.

Card 7 The Chariot

The Chariot is the first card of the Major Arcana to picture an object rather than a person or group of people. A charioteer, who controls his movement with balance and will, drives the Chariot.

The Chariot teaches us mastery and control. In a balanced and precise way, we learn to be "in the driver's seat" as we move toward our own destiny.

The Chariot is the card of the hero. As we become masters of our own destiny, we seek to help others do the same.

The Chariot can indicate travel or issues of transportation. It can also indicate forward motion, mastery, and being in control. On a more spiritual level, the Chariot can challenge us to consider what transports us to our next level. We must pursue that spiritual vehicle, whatever it may be.

The reversed Chariot may indicate car trouble, a cancelled trip, a lack of direction or being unsure of one's own abilities. You may feel stuck, that you are not moving forward.

Card 8 Strength

(Note: In some tarot traditions card eight is Justice and card eleven is Strength.)

Strength is generally shown as a woman and a lion. The woman has calmed the lion and may even control his behavior. In some images, her hand is in his mouth, in others they face each other, each waiting for the other to back down.

Strength is about taming the beast within. That beast is conquered and controlled by love, not by brute force. With this card, we learn that love is the greatest strength.

In a reading, this card may simply be a reminder that you are stronger than you think. It may also caution you to use love and gentle strength to conquer a difficult situation. It may suggest that your current position or strategy is auspicious. It may indicate an affinity for animals.

Reversed, this card can indicate anger and frustration. Something within you or around you may be out of control. Strength reversed may be a call to compassion, rather than anger.

Card 9 The Hermit

The Hermit stands alone on the mountaintop, patiently holding the lamp of knowledge for all to see.

With this card we learn to venture on our own to seek our wisdom. We also learn to share our wisdom only when asked. The Hermit teaches us the spiritual strength that comes from solitude.

While the modern Hermit holds a lantern, originally it was an hourglass in his hand. Later, he held a candle that was also a timepiece. Archetypically, he is Father Time, reminding us to be patient, and to use our time wisely.

The Hermit may represent loneliness, advanced education, or a need to seek wisdom. It may counsel silence when we wish to share wisdom that is not wanted. It instructs us to be patient with ourselves, patient with the passage of time, and patient with others.

The reversed Hermit may indicate a focus on fun and social pastimes rather than spiritual or scholarly endeavors.

Card 10 The Wheel of Fortune

In many cards the Wheel of Fortune is simply a wheel. Sometimes the Gods turn it. In some cards people or creatures ride it. In many cards it is observed by the symbols of the four gospel writers, one in each corner.

The Wheel of Fortune helps us to understand karma. We must accept that we do not always knowingly control the ups and downs of our lives. It teaches that what goes around comes around. When you are on top of the world, be prepared for a fall. When you are at the bottom, know that in time you will be lifted.

The Wheel of Fortune in a reading may represent luck. It may remind you that the hand of fate and chance will play a role in the outcome of your situation. Remember that anything can happen; you are not in control. This card refers to the gambling or taking a risk. It can refer to cycles, or something coming full circle. The karma of the past, or even a past life, may be involved.

Reversed, the Wheel of Fortune may indicate bad luck or an undesirable outcome. You may need to wait for a cycle to be completed.

Card 11 Justice

Justice is generally shown seated, holding scales in one hand and a sword in the other. In some decks she is blindfolded. In some decks her scales are in use, weighing the merits of one object against another.

Justice teaches us to be at peace with the unfairness of life. We must remember that justice will exist in the macrocosm, not in the microcosm. We must trust that justice is done even if we do not see it happen. We cannot take justice into our own hands. We must trust a higher power to tend to that, in its own time and place. And in all that, we must strive to be fair with others, even if we ourselves have not been treated fairly.

The Justice card may indicate legal matters, appearance in a court of law or official hearings or meetings. It may ask you if you are being fair or being treated fairly. It may speak of a need to keep balance within a relationship.

Reversed, this card may indicate a feeling of being treated unfairly, or a situation that is out of balance. An unfavorable outcome in court is predicted.

Card 12 The Hanged Man

A man is hung upside down by one leg. Although in an uncomfortable position, he does not show his discomfort. Rather, he is patient, meditative, and unconcerned.

The Hanged Man teaches us that when you can't change your situation, you need to change your attitude. There are times when we must surrender control or simply accept that we were never in control in the first place.

In a reading the Hanged Man may indicate a waiting period. It may suggest that you look at things with a new perspective. It may represent the need to let go, the need to relinquish control, or the need to sacrifice of oneself. It may represent the enlightenment that comes from a period of difficulty.

In its reversal, The Hanged Man may suggest a time to take control, or someone trying to control you or a situation around you.

Card 13 Death

Death is often shown as a grim figure on horseback whom none can avoid. Some modern decks have more peaceful images, and some have even changed the name of the card to "Transition" or "Transformation."

Death teaches us that change is unavoidable. The old passes away, and the new comes in. This happens to all of us, whether we are ready for it or not.

In a reading, the Death card represents a significant change. It could signify marriage, a new child, a new job or any other life change that requires a shift in perspective, attitude, expectations or behavior.

When reversed, Death may indicate stagnancy or stubbornness. In some instances, that could translate into more positive qualities like tenacity, or loyalty toward a person or ideal.

Card 14 Temperance

Usually we see Temperance pouring water from one cup to another without spilling a drop. Often, she balances one foot on water and one on land. Sometimes she is a winged angel.

Temperance is the card of alchemy. It teaches us to create the perfect blend in our lives. With patience, caution and balance we learn to mix the elements of our lives together to create a perfect harmony.

In a reading, Temperance suggests patience, balance, and caution. You may have to creatively juggle to make your life work or to solve a problem. It may caution against anger, haste, or over-indulgence.

Reversed, it may indicate a sense of impatience or imbalance. You may be having a hard time integrating aspects of your life.

Card 15 The Devil

The Devil often has two human captives chained to him. The chains are loose around their necks and their hands are free. The humans are able to remove the chains but choose not to.

The Devil is about understanding our self-imposed limitations. It requires us to examine our unhealthy behaviors and situations, and to look for positive change.

In a reading, the Devil can indicate unhealthy behaviors, attitudes or relationships. In may describe substance abuse, disease, mental health issues, addictions or abusive relationships. It may signify feeling trapped in a difficult situation.

It can also refer to appropriate commitments that sometimes seem enslaving, such as the care of a child or a sick loved one.

The reversed Devil may indicate healing and recovery. A release is indicated, such as quitting a bad habit or changing a bad situation.

Card 16 The Tower

The Tower is usually depicted as a structure stuck by lightening, with people falling to the ground below.

The lesson of the Tower is simple. That which is built on faulty foundations will be swept away, in order to build something new.

When the Tower appears in a reading, it can indicate a shake-up, a meltdown, or a potential disaster. It can also indicate the flash of inspiration that turns a disaster into a growth experience, or the opportunity for something new. The slate is wiped clean, but the process is painful.

It may indicate the removal from your life of something that needed to go that you did not have the courage to remove.

The reversed Tower may indicate that the storm has already passed, or that the shake-up will not be as bad as you expect.

Card 17 The Star

A sensuous woman in the bright starlight pours water onto water, and onto land.

The Star teaches us to graciously accept healing, abundance, and fulfillment. We learn to allow positive energy to flow around us without restriction.

In a reading, the Star can signify sensual and spiritual fulfillment, abundance, healing, and enjoyment. A traditional keyword for this card is 'hope', like wishing on a star.

Occasionally this card appears to discuss a diva-like attitude; the desire to have all of one's wishes fulfilled immediately.

The reversed Star indicates fulfillment that is somewhat delayed, or something that is less satisfying than it could be.

Card 18 The Moon

A dog, a wolf, and a crustacean are entranced by the Moon's light. A twisted path leads from the water to distant hills that seem closer to the moon.

The Moon is a card of mystery, so it is fitting that so many tarot students should find it hard to understand. Likewise, its interpretations are divergent and conflicting in many books. Perhaps the Moon's most important lesson is to look further than what your eyes can see. Objects in the moonlight appear differently than they really are. Use all your senses to perceive your situation.

In a reading, the Moon may signify mystery and confusion. It may instruct the use of magick and intuition, to harness the unseen forces. It may warn you that not all is as it seems. It might remind you to pay attention to your dreams and feelings.

The reversed Moon may indicate that you are not paying attention to spiritual matters, or that you have solved a mystery. It can also refer to inappropriate use of magick.

Card 19 The Sun

A small child perches fearlessly on a white horse, without benefit of saddle, reins or clothing. Sunflowers turn to face the child rather than facing the sun shining brightly above.

The lesson of the Sun is to allow yourself to shine. Let no fear, person or obstacle keep you from being as brilliant as you can be.

The Sun in a reading can indicate happiness, brilliance, and enjoyment. It can remind you to be all that you can be. It suggests that all truths will be brought to light. The Sun shows the beauty of a life without fear.

Occasionally this card can indicate an overblown ego; the desire to always be the center of attention.

The reversed Sun is still a positive card but suggests that there is something keeping you from your full potential.

Card 20 Judgment

One tradition for this card is to depict the Christian Judgment Day with the Angel Gabriel blowing his horn and souls rising out of coffins to greet him. Newer decks have more gentle images, such as the phoenix rising out of its ashes.

Judgment is about endings and new beginnings. It is also about the time of judging that comes when a task is completed. One of Judgment's lessons is closure. We must leave the past behind in order to progress to the future.

When Judgment appears in a reading, it may suggest the need for closure. It may discuss a project that is near completion, or a time when you are waiting for a decision. It may suggest the need for caution and clear thought as you venture on a new path. It can also be a "wake up call," or a sense of "hearing your calling." It may indicate direction communication with the voice of Spirit.

In its reversal, we may be resistant to an ending or transition, or we may need to wait for something that is taking longer than expected. We may not be hearing the spiritual message that is being given us.

Card 21 The World

Very often in this card a woman dances within a wreath of flowers. Many newer decks have used celestial images of planet Earth to depict this card.

Perhaps the greatest lesson of this card is the concept that we are all one and that all is one within us. Our goal is to reach a sense of spiritual completion.

In a reading, the World may suggest travel, or ecological or global issues affecting the Earth or the world at large. It may suggest a completion, or a victorious ending. It may portend great possibilities if your dreams are large enough. It reminds you to look at the big picture.

The reversed World can suggest that your world is turned upside down. It may also reflect a sense of incompletion, a feeling that things in your world have not yet come together the way you would like.

Major Arcana Exercises

Identifying with the Fool

Look at the Fool in your tarot deck. The traditional Fool is at a crossroads, or about to walk off a cliff. Pull a tarot card at random to describe what crossroad or cliff you might be facing at this time.

Your Fool may be in the company of a small animal. Some people see it as a guardian; others see it as the animal instinct of the Fool. What do you think this animal represents?

Your Fool may be carrying a pouch or a bag. In that pouch is said to be the Four Tools of Magick that become the suit icons of the Minor Arcana; the Sword, the Wand, the Cup and the Pentacle. Pull four tarot cards to represent the personal tools and talents that you carry with you at this time.

Key Words

Make a list of single words or short phrases that you associate with each card. Memorize these words and use them as the basis for your understanding of each card.

Meditation

Mediate on each Major Arcana card. Picture yourself in each card as the card character. Then picture yourself in a conversation with that character. What does it feel like to be each character? What does each character have to say to you?

Exercise for the Advanced Student: Best and Worst

Look through your Major Arcana card by card. Choose the Major Arcana card that appeals most to you and then the one that you like the least. Next choose the one that you have the hardest time understanding. Write about each of these cards and why you have chosen them. Now look at them again and consider the following:

The card that you like best describes some part of your personality that pleases you.

The card that you dislike most describes some part of your personality that you don't like.

The card that you have a hard time understanding describes something about yourself with which you are uncomfortable or unsure.

Write about these cards in this context. What have you learned about yourself?

CHAPTER THREE

The Minor Arcana

Lesser Secrets

The name "Minor Arcana" means "Lesser Secrets." These cards speak of the events and lessons of daily life. Our goals, our work, our relationships, our projects, our successes and failures are all illustrated in the Minor Arcana.

The Minor Arcana is divided into four suits, like playing cards. Each suit is associated with one of the four elements. The element of the suit dictates the issues and energies generally associated with the cards of the suit.

As with a standard deck of playing cards, the cards in each suit are numbered ace through ten, so each has an elemental correspondence and a numerological correspondence. These cards are called the pip cards.

Second Edition Author Note:

Since first writing this I have learned from tarot historians that, technically, the forty numbered Minor Arcana cards are only called "pips" when they are non-illustrated, as in the Tarot de Marseilles. In decks of this tradition, each of the forty numbered cards is illustrated only with the proper number of its suit icon. Decks that are considered fully-illustrated have pictures on each Minor Arcana card that may or may not include the specific number of icons, but which convey the general meaning of the card. With fully illustrated decks it is more precise to refer to these forty cards as the "numbered Minor Arcana cards".

* * *

Each suit also has a Court of four characters that are like the Jacks, Queens and Kings of regular playing cards. In tarot the Court cards are typically called Pages, Knights, Queens and Kings.

The Court cards can represent the people in our life or aspects of our own personalities. The Court cards can also predict specific occurrences and offer advice, just as the rest of the deck does.

Just as the Major Arcana tells the story of the Fool in his search for wisdom and meaning, the Minor Arcana tells the human story of the Fool in his developing understanding of each element. As you will learn in subsequent chapters, the metaphysical properties of the four elements are cornerstones of tarot understanding and spirituality.

The traditional order of the suits is Wands, Cups, Swords, and Pentacles. That is how I will present them here. For each card I will give a brief description of a popular image, generally one that was designed or inspired by A. E. Waite.

A.E. Waite designed what are still considered the most popular tarot images in the world. The original deck was drawn by Pamela "Pixie" Colman Smith, to his specifications. The deck was first published in 1910 by William Rider and Son and is thus known as the Rider-Waite-Smith deck, or RWS for short. There have been many subsequent new editions of this deck, including the Universal Waite, the Golden Rider and the Radiant Waite, to name only a few. Many tarot artists have reimagined the RWS images in different art styles or with different themes.

Second Edition Author Note:

In the past few years many respected tarotists have begun calling this deck the Waite-Smith deck, thus dropping the name of the original publisher entirely. A strong case for this nomenclature is made by Marcus Katz and Tali Goodwin in their book, *Secrets of the Waite-Smith Tarot*.

* * *

The divinatory meanings I give for each card are meant to inspire your own imagination, and to help you develop your own meanings for each card.

Second Edition Author Note:

We develop our own meanings for each card by using a variety of processes. When we journal and record our readings, we can see and document exactly how the cards play out over time.

When we spend time looking at a card, the image often speaks to us. How we feel about each image, and what we see in each card, helps us develop our own personal understanding of each card.

It's also true that your understanding of each card will change and grow over time. Just as our relationships with people get deeper as we get to know them, our relationships with the images and archetypes of tarot deepen as well.

* * *

Wands

In traditional tarot decks the suit of Wands is associated with the element of Fire. Fire corresponds with passion, creativity, and anger. The suit of Wands depicts the things that get us "fired up" or "heated" and the things that "burn in our hearts." Our creative projects, our hobbies, and our passions are all related to the suit of Wands.

In some decks the Wands are instead associated with Air. In this case they are still read as cards of creativity that is born of mental process. Our thoughts and ideas, ruled by Air, stir the passions within us.

Ace

A Wand appears in the center of the card, held by a mysterious hand or an angel. The Wand may be fiery, or it may be sprouting new, green growth.

The Ace of Wands may predict or depict a new creative project, a new hobby, a new passion or a new excitement. It may also suggest a blaze of anger.

The reversed Ace may suggest a need for passion, a creative block, or the need for a new project. There may be a lack of energy or vitality.

Two

The Two of Wands often shows a person standing on a balcony and holding a small globe. This person is dreaming of a new project and planning for the future. This card suggests a time to dream, plan, and set goals. You hold the world in your hands, what is it that you plan to do with it?

This is a card of manifestation; of thinking something into being.

When the Two of Wands is reversed, you may be forgetting to dream, plan and set goals, or your dreams may be inappropriate, or will not or did not manifest as you had hoped. It may be that you are spending too much time dreaming, and not enough time doing.

Three

The Three of Wands often shows a person standing on a cliff watching his ships come in. Perhaps the new project of the Ace and the dreams, plans, and goals of the Two have been fulfilled and now your ship is coming in! This card denotes a first success or first victory.

Reversed, it suggests that things may not be as successful as you had hoped. Or, success may be delayed. Perhaps you do not believe in your own success.

Four

Four wands form a canopy, under which a happy couple celebrates. Since four is a stable number and Fire is an unstable element, this card suggests the happy balance where passion finds a stable home. This is the traditional marriage card. It can indicate a happy home, successful projects and celebrations.

Reversed it could signify a divorce or an unhappy or unstable situation.

Five

Five people use their wands as weapons, fighting each other. The Fire energy has raged uncontrollably. There is chaos and conflict. Perhaps it is a necessary conflict, where the truth is fighting to be heard. Perhaps it is a wasteful conflict that is born of boredom, anger, misunderstanding or selfishness. Perhaps these people are working to build something together, and it is the inevitable conflict of the creative process that we see.

Reversed, we may see an avoidance of necessary conflict or a fear of conflict.

Second Edition Author Note:

In the past few years I've started seeing something more than conflict in the Five of Wands. Perhaps the five characters are playing. Perhaps they are building something. When this card appears during an in-person client session I will ask the client what they think the people are doing. So far, every client has said either playing, fighting or building. Whichever of these the client says is what they need to be doing in the situation on which the reading is focused. Whether or not you try this technique, it might be helpful for you (as it was for me) to expand your sense of the Five of Wands beyond simple conflict and embrace the possibility of play or collaboration.

***

Six

A man rides ceremoniously on a horse, surrounded by symbols of pageantry, most notably a wreath of laurels. After the conflict of the Five, we have a victorious resolution. The battle has been fought and won. This card can indicate athleticism, military service, competition or a competitive nature.

The reversed Six may indicate a loss, or a less than positive resolution. It may suggest that a person "feels like a loser" or is not presently succeeding at achieving a specific goal.

Seven

A poorly shod man successfully defends himself against attacks from all directions. This card represents the need to stand alone or the need to stand up for what one believes. It may describe a need to multitask, or to serve multiple agendas simultaneously. It describes a defensive posture and advises vigilance.

When reversed, friends will come to help when they are needed. It may be appropriate to be less defensive.

Second Edition Author Note:

In retrospect, my vague reference to the mismatched shoes of this Waite-Smith image doesn't do justice to this interesting depiction. The truth is, I had been working with this deck for many years before I noticed that the character isn't wearing matching shoes. Once I saw it, I interpreted it to mean that, as well as being hard-pressed and under duress, our hero is poorly prepared for his mission, though nonetheless successful.

In their extremely helpful book, *Secrets of the Waite-Smith Tarot*, Marcus Katz and Tali Goodwin suggest that this pictorial addition came directly from the artist, Pamela Coleman Smith. They make a convincing argument that the character is costumed as Petruchio, from Shakespeare's *The Taming of the Shrew*, arriving to his wedding intentionally poorly-dressed.

* * *

Eight

Eight wands streak through the air. We can't see where they have come from or where they are going. This card stresses motion and movement. It suggests that although the outcome is unknown, we must act out our intentions with as much creativity and strength as we can.

The Eight of Wands is a card of speed and communication. It suggests quick action and clear communication. It predicts an important message. This card can encourage you to have a difficult conversation that you've been avoiding.

Reversed, we see stagnation. Nothing is moving. In its reversal this card can indicate a serious communication problem.

Nine

A guard has fought, been wounded, and is ready to fight again. He waits patiently and stays vigilant. This card suggests patience and advises you not to drop your guard, but also to not go looking for the fight.

You have been tested and must be prepared to be tested again. The time of your testing is not of your own choosing.

Like the Major Arcana Nine, the Hermit, you stand alone.

The reversed Nine may indicate impatience or imprudence. It might also suggest that you do not need to stand alone; your friends will be there to help you.

Ten

A man carries a heavy burden toward the town. No one is there to help him, but he carries his stack of wands successfully. This card symbolizes heavy burdens that are not shared but will be carried successfully.

There may be a feeling of overwhelm indicated by this card.

Reversed, we can relinquish our burdens, at least for a while. Perhaps aid will come from those around you.

Cups

Traditionally, Cups are associated with the element of Water. Water corresponds with emotions, feelings, love, and matters of the heart. Cups cards may give insight into relationships, love affairs, family matters, feelings, and the way our emotions affect our lives.

Ace

A dove descends into a cup from which streams of water flow. A divine hand holds the cup. The Ace of Cups symbolizes the open heart. Archetypically, it is the Holy Grail. It may represent the womb of the Goddess in Pagan cultures or the womb of the Magdalene in Christian or Gnostic cultures. The Dove in the Waite image is a symbol of the Pentecost.

The Ace of Cups can predict a new love, either romantic or not. It represents the heart chakra, or the healed heart. The heart is ready to give and receive love.

The range of this card's possibilities includes everything from the new relationship vibe of an exciting crush or a first date to a prediction of marriage or parenthood to an expression of spiritual love emanating from heaven.

Reversed, the heart may be hurt, or closed. A new relationship may not work out, love may be lost. Somehow, we are not "feeling the love".

Two

The Two of Cups often pictures a happy couple drinking from their cups. This is the card of perfect love and perfect partnership. It can represent balance, union, and being at peace in one's heart.

This card may also speak of partnerships other than romantic and may also encourage you to be a good partner to yourself.

Reversed, there is imbalance. A partnership may be ill-advised. A love relationship may end.

Three

Three women dance merrily, cups in hand. I often refer to this as the "party card." It may suggest celebrations and happy occasions. This is a card of fun and social activities, and of song, dance, and laughter.

Very often, this card can speak specifically of female companionship.

Reversed, there has been too much frivolity, or not enough.

Four

A young person spurns three cups that have been offered. A fourth cup, even more special than the first three, is offered, and refused. I often call this the "spoiled child" card. You may not be happy with the options in front of you. This card may advise an attitude check or the need to make the best of a bad situation.

The Four of Cups is also a card of discernment, suggesting the need for a careful decision. Perhaps it is best to take no cup now and wait for something better.

When reversed, it suggests finding a solution, making a decision, being an optimist or making do with what is available to you.

Five

A distraught figure mourns the spilling of three cups, while two remain unnoticed and intact. There is loss and disappointment, and we are mourning our losses rather than delighting in that which remains. This is a card of pessimism or "crying over spilt milk."

This card can also indicate real grief and loss, and a legitimate and appropriate time of mourning. Even then, there is solace to be found in the two remaining cups.

The inherent advice of the Five of Cups is to focus on what you have, rather than what you have lost.

When reversed, we are making the best of a bad situation, or healing from our losses.

Six

Children make an offering of gathered flowers. This is a card that harkens to childhood, or events of the past. It speaks of happy memories, or a shared history.

This card can predict a return to your childhood home. It can tell you to look to your past to understand your present. This card can speak of past lives and soul connections.

The Six of Cups can also predict a reunion, or a gathering of old friends. It sometimes speaks of repeating a past mistake.

When reversed, we may be failing to remember the past or to honor our ancestors. Or, we may be living too much in the past and focusing too much on nostalgia.

Seven

A figure stands before seven cups in a dream-like image. Each cup holds something mysterious. This card suggests choices and decisions, as well as a fertile imagination. There is an admonition to choose carefully, because each cup holds something different, and some things are more pleasant than others.

The Seven of Cups can also suggest confusion. It speaks of a need for clarity and true information.

The reversed Seven of Cups suggests a lack of imagination, an inability to make choices, or not knowing what your options really are.

Eight

After stacking the cups on the shoreline, the figure walks into the distance. This card suggests the abandonment of successful projects. It may tell you it is time to walk away from something. You may feel abandoned or be hanging on to abandonment issues from the past.

The Eight of Cups can speak of the process of letting go of hurts from the past and walking away from sorrow.

When reversed, the Eight of Cups suggests a sense of tenacity or stubbornness.

Nine

A happy merchant surveys the nine cups that are his wares. This is a card of happiness and fulfillment. Traditionally, it is the "Wish Card." It predicts that your wishes and desires will come to fruition.

Although the suit of Cups is about emotion, this card can indicate success in business ventures.

Reversed, there may be dissatisfaction and frustration.

Ten

A happy family frolics under a rainbow. This is often called "The Happy Family." It can indicate family unity, happiness, a happy home, love, fertility, and happy endings.

When reversed, this card can indicate a lack of harmony in the home, problems in a relationship, or the end of a relationship.

Swords

In most decks, Swords are associated with the element of Air, and rule the powers of the mind. Swords are associated with our thoughts, ideas, integrity and communication. They also describe our anxiety and worries.

In some decks, Swords are associated with the element of Fire. In this case they still refer to the mind, but the imagery is different. The mind imagery of Air focuses on clarity, the cleansing breath and the true word. The mind imagery of Fire focuses on the flash of creative inspiration that sparks from within.

Swords are often considered the most difficult cards to receive in a reading. Many of their images and interpretations can be painful, as facing the truth usually is. It's helpful to remember that the Swords represent the thoughts, ideas and words that we allow to hurt us.

Ace

A powerful hand presents a sharp sword from which hangs the crown and laurels of successful battle. The Ace of Swords signifies a new truth, a new idea, a new understanding, or a new way of thinking. It may also suggest new knowledge, or information recently revealed.

The Ace of Swords can also symbolize the essence of truth, or the communication of truth.

The Ace of Swords commands us to do the right thing, and to speak our truth.

The reversed Ace of Swords may indicate dishonesty, mistrust or lack of thought.

Two

A woman sits in front of rocky waters. She is blindfolded and balances two swords on her shoulders, uses them to cross off her heart.

Each sword represents an idea, or a direction. She balances between them, perhaps weighting her choices, trying to decide.

Aleister Crowley's keyword for this card is "Peace." Be at peace with the need to make decisions, or with your own indecision. Look inward to choose your path. Use your mind rather than your heart to pick your direction.

Reversed, this may suggest a decision that you do not want to make, or a sense of disquiet.

Three

Three swords pierce a heart against a dark background. This is traditionally the card of the lover's triangle. It can represent sorrow, heartache, treachery, and betrayal. It suggests a wound that requires healing.

In its reversal, healing and recovery have already begun.

Four

Swords hang in the air while a knight finds his resting place. This card suggests meditation. It advises withdrawal from daily life. Rest and retreat are indicated. This is time to lay down your swords. You may need time to recover. There may be a feeling of emptiness, or diminished possibilities.

When reversed, the Four suggests a busy time. There may be a need to exert a great deal of energy. You may feel that you need to run on borrowed energy for a short-but-intense time.

Five

A battle is enjoined. We can see a winner and a loser.

This card suggests the need to prepare for a battle that cannot or should not be avoided. There will be a clear winner and loser. This card does not predict who the victor will be. This card simply tells you to give the battle your all and fight to win.

This card may also describe the aftermath of a battle already fought, or an ongoing battle within oneself.

Reversed, there is a way to resolve differences with diplomacy. The reversed Five of Swords may describe a person as being diplomatic. It could also suggest a strategy that involves compromise.

Six

In the Waite image we see a family sailing toward smoother waters.

Aleister Crowley's keyword for this card is "Science."

When we put these two tarot traditions together, we can see that the Six of Swords brings a message of clarity. It tells us that clear thinking, and focusing on logic over emotion, can speed our journey from chaos to calm.

Because of the Waite depiction, this card is traditionally said to predict a journey over water.

While this isn't a joyous card, its general mood is one of improvement and forward motion. It encourages logically thinking and sound strategy.

It its reversal, this card may describe a sense of stagnation. You may be stuck in a way of thinking that is limiting you.

Seven

A man sneaks away with swords. Traditionally, this is the "Thief's Card." It can suggest treachery and dishonesty. Someone may be lying to you, or you may be lying to yourself.

The Seven of Swords may ask you to examine your own trust issues.

This card can suggest a sense of guilt, or a feeling of getting away with something. It may tell you that problems must be solved in a crafty manner.

When reversed, this card suggests honesty, trust and integrity, or healing from a betrayal of trust.

Eight

A woman is bound and blindfolded, trapped in a cage of swords. This card can speak of bondage or addiction It can suggest a feeling of being stuck. The cage of swords can represent the fears, worries, or words which trap us. Since our thoughts have trapped us, this card also indicates that a new way of thinking can free us.

When reversed, there is a new way of thinking or a recovery from anxiety.

Nine

A despairing person is unable to sleep. This can be a card of nightmares, insomnia or sleep disturbances. It can also refer to depression, anxiety, and worry. The thoughts that have trapped us in the previous card now torment us.

Reversed, we may be recovering from worry and depression or may be overreacting to difficult news.

Ten

Clearly the most disturbing image in many tarot decks, the ten is often pictured as a figure that has been impaled with ten swords. The sun is in the distance, either rising or setting. In this card, our thoughts and fears have taken us to the worst place they can. There is pain, either physical or emotional. And there is trouble, either real or imagined. The key point here is that the damage is done, and must now be assessed objectively, and with clarity.

When reversed, we may see a sense of recovery, or a sense that the situation is not a dire as we had feared.

Pentacles

Pentacles are associated with the element of Earth. They represent material and physical things, such as money and health. They also represent grounding and stability. Hearth and home, resources of all types, family cycles, career, mastery and apprenticeship, working the land and working with our hands are all associated with the suit of Pentacles.

Ace

A hand cradles a pentacle above an inviting garden. The Ace of Pentacles represents new money, a new job, a new sense of grounding and stability, or even a new baby. This is the root chakra. It may speak to our sense of well-being.

Reversed, it may speak of instability, financial loss or a lack of grounding.

Two

A juggler handles two Pentacles within a lemniscate – the traditional infinity symbol that looks like a figure eight on its side. This signifies his ability to keep juggling for as long as he needs to. In the background are stormy seas, but he, like the ships, continues.

This card suggests the need, and the ability, to juggle time, money, or other resources. It may indicate more than one job, or many responsibilities.

Reversed, there may be too much of a drain on resources to continue at present.

Three

A craftsman is being paid and admired for his work. Many see this as the card of the "Master Craftsman", though some tarotists see him instead as an apprentice. The Three of Pentacles suggests career success and recognition. It may suggest a successful career path that is creative in nature, or one that earns the respect of the community.

When reversed, this card may indicate the loss of a job, of the lack of a career path. There may be job dissatisfaction, or the need to discover ones' calling.

Four

A man clings to his four coins. This can be the card of the miser, suggesting selfishness or pettiness. It may also suggest a time of limited resources, and therefore the need to conserve. It may advise pulling in and taking care of oneself, either financially or physically.

Sometimes the Four of Pentacles can advise the need for good boundaries.

When the Four of Pentacles is reversed, it may refer to generosity, charity, and sharing. There may also be a warning about poor boundaries.

Five

Decrepit people walk through the snow, passing the church where they could receive food, shelter and enlightenment. This is the card of the missed opportunity. It can suggest a fear that you've "missed the boat," or may describe one who does not act on their own behalf.

This card may suggest a feeling of being excluded or left out in the cold. There may be a reality or perception of poverty.

Reversed, this card suggests a willingness to be open-minded and proactive toward finding resources and opportunities.

Six

A wealthy person bestows charity to the needy with one hand but holds a scale in the other.

Traditionally, this is the card of charity. It can represent abundance, generosity, and a desire to help others. The scale represents the need to give neither too much nor too little.

Reversed, either selfishness or a lack of abundance may be indicated.

Seven

A tired gardener rests for a moment while tending his land. This is a card of tiredness, and hard work. It suggests that the garden will bear fruit at the proper time. In the meanwhile, rest when you can and work when you must.

Reversed, you may need to pay more attention to your business affairs to better "tend your garden." There may be a loss of money or career.

Eight

A person manufactures a series of pentacles. This is the card of the apprentice, of learning through hard work. It may suggest a repetitive job or an actual apprenticeship or job training program.

Some readers see mastery rather than apprenticeship in this card.

Reversed, there may be a need for training, or a problem with getting the schooling that is needed. Work may be tiring, or you may be in danger of giving up or losing your position.

Nine

A woman stands alone in her garden with her falcon. This is the card of inheritance, family money, or personal security. It suggests the ability to be comfortable and serene in solitude.

Interestingly, in recent years this has card has come to symbolize feminine independence. That is, women who are happy to be single, or who do not feel the need for romance.

This is somewhat ironic given that the security of the depicted woman originally came from her father's protection.

Reversed, there may be a sense of insecurity, either personally, emotionally or financially.

Ten

A grandfather is at home, surrounded by his family. In the Waite design, the ten pentacles are arranged to form the Kabalistic Tree of Life. This is the traditional card of the castle, and can suggest issues of house, home or real estate. It is also the card of family legacy and ancestry. It can suggest a happy and prosperous home.

Reversed, there may be problems with either the physical structure of the house, the relationships within the home, or the finances of the family. Family traditions may be dishonored.

Pip Card Exercises

Four Elements Reading

Separate your Minor Arcana ace through ten into its four suits. You should have four piles containing ten cards each. Shuffle each pile independently, and randomly pull one card from each pile. Each card chosen will represent how you are relating to that element in your life at this time.

Storytelling

Lay out ace through ten of each suit in order. Look at each suit and see the "story" of the suit. Going card by card, write a story for each suit. Use the Fool as your central character. Begin your story with the ace and end it with the ten. You can be as fanciful, or as funny, or as spiritual as you like. What does the Fool experience in each card, and in each suit?

Now, look at the cards starting with the tens, and going, in reverse order, to the aces. What stories can you tell this way?

Runs

Put your Minor Arcana suits in order, ace through ten. Within each suit, look at the progression from one card to another. What stories can you tell when you look at a progression of just three cards? Can you think of different times in your own life that could be illustrated by a numeric progression of three cards within the same suit?

Exercise for the Advanced Student-Four Elements

To understand the Four Elements, you much experience them. Swim, or walk in the rain, sit in front of a roaring fire, plant a garden in the fertile earth, fly a kite, and go for a walk on a windy day. No amount of study or meditation can replace these experiences. But how do we relate the feelings and energy of these experiences to the tarot?

Look through your pip cards and pick out three cards from each suit that you think best express the energy of each suit's element.

Meditate on the cards you have chosen and try to connect with each element by thinking about its physical attributes. Think of water as wet and cool, air as brisk and refreshing, fire as hot and bright, earth as solid and grounding. Think about the smells that you associate with each element. Perhaps you associate the smell of a spring rain, or the salt ocean, with water? Can you remember the smell of a crackling wood fire? What about the smell of rich soil in the spring? Could the smell of clothes dried on a clothesline remind you of air?

After meditating on the cards that you have chosen, write a few words about each card, and how it expresses the energy of its element.

How does each card help you to experience and understand its element?

CHAPTER FOUR

The Court of the Minor Arcana

The sixteen Court cards can be depicted and interpreted in a variety of ways. The most popular Court hierarchy is the one that appears in the tarot designed by A. E. Waite. In that design, each Court contains a Page, Knight, Queen and King, in that order. The Thoth Tarot, designed by Aleister Crowley, uses Pages, Princes, Queens and Knights, respectively.

Some modern tarot artists and authors have made an appropriate effort to make the tarot more gender-balanced and less hierarchical. Pages and Knights have become Sons and Daughters, or Seers and Seekers. Kings and Queens are renamed Mothers and Fathers, Priestesses and Shamans, or Teachers and Masters.

No matter what they are called, the Court cards can represent people. They can describe personalities or types of people that surround the querent, or they can represent aspects of the querent's personality.

The way the characters of the Court are described may change from reader to reader, or even from reading to reading. There are many methods for ascribing characteristics to each Court card. No matter what method you use, it is always good to be flexible. If a Court card makes you think of a specific person, go with what you feel. If you read with several different decks, your interpretations for each Court member may differ according to the way you react to the picture in each deck.

For me, Pages and Knights usually represent younger people, or older people who are learning or experiencing new things. Kings and Queens represent mature people. Generally, Kings are male, and Queens are female, but not always. Tradition ascribes the female gender to Pages and male to Knights, but I rarely see it that way.

Pages tend to be messengers or students, those who are curious and those who communicate. Knights are seekers and travelers, movers and shakers. Queens are nurturers and creators, and Kings are leaders and authority figures.

Some tarot traditions suggest that physical characteristics such as hair and eye color can be ascribed to specific Court cards. Others use astrology, ascribing those born under Water signs to Cups, those born under Earth signs to Pentacles, those born under Fire signs to Wands (or Swords, depending on the deck), and Air signs to Swords (or Wands).

Many readers use the characteristics of the element of each suit to ascribe personality. Cups people have Water personalities and may be sensitive, poetic, loving, and emotional. Swords people have Air personalities and may be honest communicators, rational, and logical. Wands people are fiery and may be passionate, creative, funny, and explosive. The earthy Pentacles folk are practical, hardworking, grounded, and stable.

We know that Court cards can represent people or aspects of people. We know that they can represent the querent or people surrounding the querent. But Court cards can also represent an energy that is present or that needs to be embraced by the querent. Court cards can also predict specific events.

So, how do you know if a Court card should be interpreted as an individual person, an aspect of a person, energy to be embraced, an action to be taken, or a predicted event? Here, it is important to use your intuition, and to remember that one card can often mean more than one thing at once. For instance, the Page of Wands may describe your querent's young child as being funny, precocious, verbal, temperamental, and creative. At the same time, it may also suggest that, since your querent is busy with the energy-draining work of parenting such a child, your querent also needs to learn to have fun, focus on her own creativity, and better communicate her own needs. All these ideas are communicated by that one card, The Page of Wands.

When thinking about the different things that Court cards can indicate beyond specific people and personalities, consider the following possibilities.

Pages represent communication, and may predict a letter, phone call, or email. The suit may suggest the sort of message you will receive. For instance, the Page of Pentacles predicts communication about money or career, or money in the mail. The Pages of Cups might predict a love letter. The Page of Swords may describe a missive that reveals the truth. And those concert tickets you've been waiting for, or the paints you've ordered to begin a new project, may be the Page of Wands.

Pages may also show up to remind us to communicate. Then, the suit may suggest the sort of things we need to say. Perhaps we need to have an honest talk with our roommate about finances; that could be indicated by the Page of Pentacles. Perhaps we have some anger that we need to express. That could show up as the Page of Wands. Perhaps we need to communicate love, and to really open our heart to someone. That would be the Page of Cups. If we need to reveal a truth, perhaps even a difficult truth, the Page of Swords may appear.

In the age of the internet, many readers are finding that the Pages are coming up to represent web pages! Perhaps the Page of Cups could represent internet dating, or the Page of Pentacles may suggest that an entrepreneur needs a better web presence.

Sometimes, too, when a Page appears in a reading, I tell the querent that they are being "paged" by the universe, because, in that reading, it feels like direct spiritual communication.

Pages are also students. They may represent people of any age who are learning something new. The suit, of course, may give us a clue as to what they are learning. The Pages may also tell us what we need to learn, or what we need to embrace. The Page of Wands may tell us to learn to have some fun, or to take up a new creative hobby. The Page of Swords may suggest learning to be more honest, or to be a better student. The Page of Cups may come up to teach us to have a more open heart. The Page of Pentacles may have a practical lesson for us.

Knights represent motion, advancement, and proactive measures. The Knight of Pentacles may predict advancement in career. The Knight of Swords may predict advancement in the understanding of a significant truth. The Knight of Cups may predict forward motion in a love relationship. The Knight of Wands may suggest advancement of a creative or recreational project.

Sometimes Knights appear to tell us to "get off our butts" and get moving. The Knight of Cups may tell us to take the next step in a love relationship. The Knight of Wands may be instructing the querent to take their skills and abilities to a public forum. The Knight of Swords says that integrity and truth are paramount. The Knight of Pentacles suggests unwavering pursuit of career and financial stability.

Knights may also literally predict travel. The type of travel may be determined by the suit. For instance, the Knight of Cups may be a romantic getaway. The Knight of Pentacles may be a business trip. The Knight of Wands may be a fishing trip or some other trip to pursue a fun hobby. The Knight of Swords may be an educational trip, or a retreat to clear your mind.

Queens represent nurturing qualities. They may tell us to nurture specific aspects of ourselves, or to pay attention to certain aspects of our lives. Queens may suggest that special care should be taken, especially in the area suggested by the suit. If you are reading for a woman and a few Queens show up, they may certainly represent the women around her. But they may also each represent an aspect of herself, and her search for personal identity.

Kings represent qualities of leadership and the achievement of goals. Kings may instruct us to take leadership and responsibility, to assume some authority position that we have been avoiding. They may come up to affirm our strength and ability, especially in the area suggested by the suit. Multiple Kings in a man's reading may discuss the many aspects of his personality, or his own search for personal identity and integration.

When Court cards appear in reversed positions, they may indicate people who are not able to be or to do what you would expect if they were upright. For instance, the reversed Knight of Cups may be too shy to pursue love. The reversed King of Swords may be a poor communicator or even dishonest. The reversed Queen of Cups may suffer from depression.

The reversal may indicate a temporary problem or concern, or a more permanent personality trait. Reversed Court cards can also indicate the querent's unwillingness to do what the card suggests. For instance, the reversed Kings may suggest taking a leadership role that the querent may feel uncomfortable about doing.

Meet the Court

Page of Wands

The Page of Wands stands as if ready to make a proclamation or give a performance. The Page of Wands may represent a young person who is creative or athletic with a good sense of humor and a warm heart.

The Page of Wands may refer to creative inspiration, the study of a creative field, or pursuing a passion.

Reversed, the Page of Wands may suggest a young person who is apathetic, or not using their skills and abilities. It may also suggest an avoidance of either education or communication.

Knight of Wands

The Knight of Wands rides on his horse. In some decks his horse is way too small for him. He may represent a young person who is motivated and creative, but he may also represent one who is self-important or overblown.

The Knight of Wands may direct the querent to pursue a passion, or to pursue creativity or recreation. It may suggest advancement in a wonderful career. It may also predict or suggest fun and exciting travel.

Reversed, the Knight of Wands may describe an unmotivated young person. It may also describe a cancelled trip, or a lack of energy.

Queen of Wands

The Queen of Wands is often shown with a black cat and sunflowers. The cat represents her intuition, and the sunflowers show her brilliance. She is a woman who is creative, funny, warm, and passionate.

The Queen of Wands may also represent the need to nurture creativity or passion.

Reversed, the Queen of Wands is a "Peg Bundy" type; a lazy woman of little warmth, intelligence or creativity.

It may also indicate a need to discover one's passion or creativity.

King of Wands

The King of Wands is shown as a regal authority. He represents a man who is a strong leader with a good sense of humor and a warm heart. He can be passionate, creative, and a lover of nature.

The King of Wands may suggest or predict a position of authority or a leadership role, especially in a creative project. It may also represent a professional craftsperson.

Reversed, the King of Wands is "Al Bundy." An unmotivated man, or a man who has not found his passion or has few talents. It may also suggest an unwillingness to take a leadership role, especially in a creative project, or an area of passion for the querent.

Second Edition Author Note:
I struggled with whether I should keep the Peg and Al Bundy references. There was a time that everyone in a tarot class would laugh at this and understand the cards better because of it. Now, the televi-

sion show "Married with Children" feels trite and outdated to me. I decided to keep it as a fun historical reference, if nothing else.

The practice of comparing tarot cards to pop culture characters continues to be a fun yet profound way of learning and understanding the cards.

* * *

Page of Cups

The Page of Cups proffers a cup which holds a fish. This card can represent a young person who is sensitive, kind, and poetic.

The Page of Cups may also be interpreted as a "message of love," on either a spiritual level or a romantic level. It offers an opportunity to open the heart to love and suggest communication regarding emotional issues.

Reversed, the Page of Cups may indicate a shy person, or a young person with emotional issues. It may also indicate one who is not ready or does not know how to love.

Knight of Cups

The Knight of Cups is riding toward something or someone and bringing his cup as a gift. This is the traditional card of the suitor or the "Knight in Shining Armor." It represents the pursuit of love.

This card could come up to encourage one to be a suitor or to let one know of an imminent potential suitor.

The Knight of Cups reminds us all to pursue love as the most important gift of all.

Reversed, The Knight of Cups may indicate a failed attempt at a relationship, or unwillingness to pursue love.

Queen of Cups

The Queen of Cups sits serenely by the ocean. She may represent a sensitive woman, a woman who is kind and loving, or a woman who is very emotional.

The Queen of Cups may value her own comfort highly but may also seek to make others comfortable.

The Queen of Cups may come up to tell us to nurture our own emotions, to be kind to ourselves, and to listen to our inner voice.

Reversed, the Queen of Cups may refer to a woman who is depressed or having emotional issues. It may also suggest that one is not honoring one's emotional needs or the emotional needs of others.

King of Cups

The King of Cups sits on his ocean throne, surrounded by sea life. He may represent a kind man who loves without fear and is emotionally healthy and sensitive to the needs of others.

The King of Cups may tell us that we need to set the emotional tone in a family group or love relationship. It suggests that we exercise our emotional capacity and be sensitive to the needs of others.

The reversed King of Cups may represent a man who is emotionally immature or limited. He may be unable to address his own emotional needs or incapable of expressing his emotions.

Page of Swords

The Page of Swords waves his sword in the air, brandishing it with focus and clear intent. He may represent a young person who is a sharp thinker or a wise communicator. He may represent a student at any age or one who is seeking to expand communication or intellect.

The Page of Swords tells us that we need to communicate honestly and effectively. Alternatively, it may tell us to pay attention to scholarly matters.

Reversed, The Page of Swords may represent a dishonest young person, or a lack of thought, preparation, communication, or study.

Knight of Swords

The Knight of Swords rides forward swiftly, with his sword drawn. He may represent a youthful person in pursuit of an intellectual goal or in pursuit of truth and justice.

The Knight of Swords may tell us to pursue honesty, fairness, or wisdom. He comes up to remind us to "do the right thing." This is the card of swiftness and recommends quick thought and action.

Reversed, the Knight of Swords may represent laziness, stagnation, or a lack of direction.

Queen of Swords

The Queen of Swords sits quietly, contemplating the sword in her hands. She represents a strong, wise woman. The Queen of Swords often represents a woman alone or a woman who speaks her mind freely.

The Queen of Swords may tell us to find strength from past difficulties. It may tell us to nurture open communication, and to preserve the truth at all costs.

Reversed, the Queen of Swords may speak of dishonesty or may describe a woman who is sharp-tongued or untrustworthy.

King of Swords

The King of Swords sits on his throne and surveys his kingdom. He represents a wise leader, intellectual strength, and fair decisions.

The King of Swords may appear when we need to make wise choices. He encourages us to take a leadership role and to use logic and reason in all our communication.

Reversed, he may represent a man who is dishonest, of limited intelligence or a poor communicator. A lack of leadership or a lack of clear thought may create problems.

Page of Pentacles

The Page of Pentacles proudly holds his icon. He represents an industrious child or a practical and career-minded student.

The Page of Pentacles may describe a focus on learning practical matters or learning a skill or trade.

Reversed, the Page of Pentacles may represent an unmotivated student, or a lack of work, money, goals, or discipline.

Knight of Pentacles

The Knight of Pentacles sits on his horse in full armor, holding his icon in front of him. He represents a person in pursuit of wealth and security.

In a reading, the Knight of Pentacles may describe the pursuit of career advancement or financial success.

Reversed, The Knight of Pentacles may indicate career difficulties or financial trouble.

Queen of Pentacles

The Queen of Pentacles is surrounded by symbols of nature and fertility. She indicates a mother figure or a woman who is competent in matters of home and business.

The Queen of Pentacles may suggest the need to nurture or to be nurtured when she appears in a reading. She may represent a mother or mothering issues.

Reversed, she may show up as a sign of infertility, difficulties between mother and child, or problems within the home or business.

King of Pentacles

The King of Pentacles sits on his woodland throne, surrounded by nature. He represents a firm and responsible man who is good in business.

When the King of Pentacles appears in a reading, he may indicate success in business or the need to become a leader within your profession. He suggests qualities of responsibility, stability, leadership, and discipline.

Reversed, it may indicate financial woes, job problems, or a lack of stability.

Correspondences of the Court

There are traditional correspondences for gender, element, astrology and numerology of the Court.

When contemplating gender, Pages and Queens are feminine, Knights and Kings are Masculine. That means that the Page of Cups and the Page of Pentacles are feminine/feminine, while the Page of Wands and the Page of Swords are feminine/masculine.

This will usually not reflect on gender, gender preferences or orientation of the querent. It may show whether an individual is nurturing yin or yang energies more predominately or keeping a balance between the two.

There are elemental associations for each of the Court as well. When the Court cards appear to represent people, the people they indicate may be born under zodiacal signs associated with the element of the suit. In other words, Cups people may be born under Water signs (Cancer, Scorpio, Pisces). Wands people may be born under Fire signs (Aries, Leo, Sagittarius). Air people may be born under Air signs (Gemini, Libra, Aquarius), while Earth people may be born under Earth signs (Taurus, Virgo, Capricorn).

There is also a tarot tradition that associates Earth with Pages, Air with Knights, Water with Queens and Fire with Kings. This gives us further insight into the personalities and energies of the Court cards.

We see the Page of Pentacles as "Earth of Earth," making him a particularly strong and grounded young student. The Page of Swords, as "Earth of Air" may have the best of both worlds in that he is grounded to the Earth and expansive in his thinking. On the other hand, he may have to work to keep on task, and may occasionally speak out of turn because of the Air energy that tugs him away from his natural grounding.

The Knight of Swords, as "Air of Air" is the speediest of the Knights – quick acting and sharp thinking. The Knight of Pentacles, though, is a bit of a conundrum. As an airy Knight, he wants to move quickly, but as the Knight of Earth, or "Air of Earth," he is more grounded, and more cautious.

The Queen of Cups, as "Water of Water" is ultra-dreamy, and maybe sometimes overly emotional. The Queen of Pentacles, as "Water of Earth" is the perfect nurturer, able to bring forth life in abundance.

The King of Wands is "Fire of Fire." This makes him the most passionate and creative of all the Kings. But the King of Cups is "Fire of Water." He may sometimes limit himself, or stand in the way of his own success, in the way that water douses fire. However, if the King of Cups can balance the elements of Fire and Water within himself he becomes a passionate and considerate lover and leader.

Second Edition Author Note:

I have since come to understand that the elemental associations I have learned for the four Court ranks is but one tradition. Many tarotists use different elemental associations for the ranks than the ones I have listed here. As with most things tarot, work with the associations that resonate best for you.

* * *

There are several traditions regarding numerology and the Court. One way is to count the Page as One, the Knight as Two, the Queen as Three, and the Kings as Four. We could then compare Pages to Aces, and to the Magician. Knight could be compared to Twos, and to the High Priestess. For the Queens, we could look at the Threes and the Empress. For the Kings, we could look at the Fours and the Emperor.

Another way is to count the Pages as two, the Knight as three, and so forth. In that case, the Pages would bring the energy of the twos, and the High Priestess, the Knights would correspond with the threes and the Empress, The Queens with the fours and the Emperor and the Kings with the fives and the Hierophant.

From my perspective, neither of these systems work perfectly. Of course, to make the Queens threes and the Kings fours makes perfect sense. But the action-oriented Knights seem a bit out of place as twos.

On the other hand, Pages are perfect twos in their contemplative nature, and Knights are good threes in their tendency to produce and push forward. But relating Queens to the Emperor rather than the Empress is a bit of a stretch for me.

Perhaps the value of these systems is simply in our ability to play with them. The more we discuss the possibilities, the more we develop a solid understanding of tarot numerology, and of the characters of the Court.

Court Card Exercises

Key Words

Look at all sixteen Court cards and think of them as people. Make lists of key words for their personality traits. Now look at each card reversed, and list those personality traits.

Significator

Decide whether you are a Page, a Knight, a King, or a Queen. Now, look at your astrological sign and see which suit is related to your element. Now you know which card, by tradition, would signify you. Are you comfortable with that, or is there another card that seems to fit you better? Why?

People in Your Life

Think of three people you know and write down their names. Chose a Court card, either right side up or reversed, to represent each of them. Explain why you chose each card for each person.

What to Do?

Think about each Court card as communicating a verb. Pages suggest that we learn and communicate. Knights suggest that we pursue and travel. Queens suggest that we nurture or create. Kings suggest that we take authority and lead. The suits, of course, suggest the arena in which we need to take these actions.

Shuffle the sixteen Court cards. Ask the universe to give you guidance on what you need to be doing currently in your life. Pick one Court card at random to give you that answer.

Numbers Exercise

Look at each tradition of numerology and the Court presented in the last section. Which one makes the most sense to you, and why?

Exercise for the Advanced Student- Expand the Role of Tarot in Your Life

Tarot can be used for many purposes and can be helpful in many ways. Shuffle your entire tarot deck and think about tarot in your life. Ask the question, "How has tarot been helping me in my life?" and pull a card. Now ask the question, "In what ways can tarot help me that I haven't considered?" and pull another card. Look at the two cards, and see how they relate to the questions, and how they relate to each other.

CHAPTER FIVE

Perspectives on Tarot

There are many ways to understand tarot, and many ways to use tarot cards. Over the years, tarot scholars have developed perspectives on tarot that have become part of modern tarot understanding. For instance, before Eden Gray coined the term "Fool's Journey" to refer to the Major Arcana, no one understood the Major Arcana as the journey of the Fool. Now, every tarot student is introduced to this perspective.

As you study different perspectives of tarot, remember that your own developing perspective is just as important as any you will learn in a book.

Four Methods of Tarot Reading

When I first began my tarot studies, I learned that there are four methods of tarot reading. These methods are interpretive, intuitive, psychological, and archetypal.

Interpretive readings simply require you to interpret the cards that come up according to their traditional meanings. The amazing thing to me, as a new student, was that the cards would so often come up in a way that fit perfectly. Years later, I am still in awe of the uncanny accuracy of the cards themselves.

Intuitive reading uses the cards as a tool to increase psychic awareness. Early on it became clear to me that by holding the cards in my hands I gave myself permission to feel and speak my intuition. The pictures and symbols in the cards often awaken ideas and give rise to clear vision. Sometimes these ideas are not the ideas that are traditionally associated with a particular card, but still they are accurate in the particular reading. Sometimes intuition adds to the interpretation, giving deeper meaning or additional information.

Psychological reading uses the tarot images to illustrate and give words to feelings and situations that the client is experiencing. This method allows me to ask a client, "Which one of these cards do you find particularly disturbing?" Or, I might show the client a graphic card and explain it to her in reference to her own life. "Here," I might say, "is a picture of you. Do you see that you are bound and blindfolded and stuck in a cage?" Then the client and I can figure out why she is there and what she can do about it.

Sometimes a querent is struck by a card's image. She may feel drawn to it, repulsed by it, or curious about it. Understanding the feelings the image invokes can provide critical insight to the reading.

Archetypal tarot is based on the idea that each card is an archetype, a symbol that we can all understand. Each card represents a theme, character, experience, or lesson that we will all encounter at some point within our lifetime. Looking at the cards this way allows us to see the commonality of our human experience. It allows us to relate the cards to situations and symbols in our own lives. It is helpful for us to be able to say, "My father is the Hierophant," or, "I'm having a Five of Pentacles sort of a day."

Intuitive Exercise

Pull three cards as a reading for yourself, but do not interpret them. Instead, take your tarot notebook and write down all the images that you see in each card. Focus only on the images and not on the meanings of the cards. Now, think about those images and let your mind wander. Write down the things you think about. Read over what you've written. How does it relate to what is going on in your life?

Exercise for the Advanced Student- Interpretive Reading

Pull three cards as a reading for yourself. Write down all the key words and phrases you know for all three cards. Here, you are focusing on the meanings of the cards as you've learned them. Put the cards away and look at all the words and phrases that you have written. How do they fit together to create ideas, sentences or paragraphs? How do these correlate with what is really going on in your life?

Five Ways to See Tarot

After two decades of working with tarot, I feel there are at least five ways of seeing and describing tarot as a whole.

1. *Tarot is a book of spiritual lessons.*
2. *Tarot is a language.*
3. *Tarot is a tool for stimulating creativity.*
4. *Tarot is a means of communicating with the spirit world.*
5. *Tarot is a set of magickal tools.*

Lady Frieda Harris, illustrator of the Thoth Tarot, referred to the tarot as "God's picture book." Indeed, tarot is a book of spiritual wisdom, much like the Holy Bible, the Koran, or the Tao Te Ching. However, tarot is a book that tells its stories entirely in pictures. As we learn tarot, it is important that we learn more than simply what meanings are associated with each card when they come up in a reading. We need to see the lesson of each card. We must learn what the Fool learns at each stop in his journey.

Many tarot readers and authors have compared tarot to a language. Some tarot spreads are read as a sentence. I often ask my tarot students to decide if a particular card is acting as a noun, a verb or as an adjective within a spread. For example, the Eight of Wands might be an adverb, saying that something happens 'quickly'. The Knight of Swords could mean the same thing, but could also be a noun, describing a person. It could also be a verb, describing an action such as movement or travel.

Tarot cards symbolize more than just words. They symbolize our deepest fears, our greatest hopes, and our most noble ambitions. Sometimes the cards speak more than words ever will and give us the ability to understand and communicate the depth of our feelings at a soul level. Suppose you had never before seen a tarot deck and someone showed you the Tower, or the Sun, and suggested that was how they were feeling. You would inherently know what that person was experiencing and remember times when you had been there yourself.

Tarot is a wonderful example of creativity and a wonderful tool for creative inspiration. Creative people all have a similar complaint at one point or another. We feel stale or blocked. Suddenly and without warning, a creative person becomes seemingly unable to have an original idea. Simply pulling tarot cards can bring us out of our block and give ideas, focus, and direction.

Carl Jung suggested that the tarot was a means for the subconscious mind to communicate with the conscious mind. It is also a means for us to communicate with our ancestors, spirit guides and departed loved ones. It is an easy exercise to call on an entity in spirit and ask, "what message do you have for me?" then pull a card. Sometimes the answer is clear. Sometimes the answer will require meditation and soul-searching. But the images that you are given will always speak truth from the spirit world.

Your tarot deck is a pack of magickal tools that can be used to invoke spiritual energies or to create change. For instance, a Minor Arcana card can be used to invoke the element of its suit. Major Arcana cards such as the Empress or the Hermit can be used to invoke the male and female aspects of divinity.

Tarot magick works on the magickal theory that "like attracts like." If you want to attract something into your life, choose a tarot card that represents your desire. Meditate on that image, keep it on your tarot altar, or carry it with you. You can even print out a copy of the image to hang on your wall. The energy that is represented by the card will be drawn to you.

You can also use tarot magick to banish something that no longer serves you. If you wanted to cure yourself of anxiety, for instance, you could look at the Eight of Swords. In meditation, you could imagine yourself as the subject of this card. How can you remove yourself from this position? In your mind go through the motions of freeing yourself.

You can also find cards to represent energies that you want to remove from your life, print out copies of those images and destroy those copies in ceremony. As you destroy the image, you are destroying whatever it represents in your life.

As you can see, tarot is a versatile and dynamic tool on our spiritual journey. There are many ways to view tarot and many ways to use tarot. As we embrace tarot as a tool on our spiritual journey, it is important not to limit ourselves.

Tarot Tool Exercise

Shuffle the cards and talk to them. Ask them, "what can you do for me today?" and pull a card. In what way does the card suggest tarot can help you today?

Holistic Tarot

We often hear reference to "body, mind and spirit." Most of us recognize this to mean a holistic view of life. We need to take care of ourselves on all three of these levels. All three levels are intertwined. What's going on in our thoughts affects our health and well-being. What's going on spiritually affects our physical and mental health. As we nurture our bodies, we have greater spiritual attunement and greater mental clarity.

We also need to remember that life happens on all three levels. A goal of the spiritual journey is to master the challenges of body, mind, and spirit during our physical lifetime. Tarot is a tool that can help us understand our physical and material realities. It can give us appropriate information related to work, well-being, and our mundane responsibilities. Thus, it pertains to the body and to the material world. Tarot also helps us find clarity of mind. It can help us separate fact from fiction and set priorities. It can offer perspective in decision-making. It can help us process our feelings and lead us to emotional healing. Therefore, it pertains to the mind and the emotional world. Tarot is also a roadmap for our spiritual journey. It helps us to understand our spiritual nature and achieve our spiritual goals. It is even a tool for communicating with the spirit world.

And so, we see that tarot can give information that nurtures the body, mind, and spirit.

One way of viewing the Fool's Journey through the Major Arcana is to ascribe cards one (ace) through seven to the body, or to the material world, cards eight through fourteen to the mind, or to the emotional world, and cards fifteen through twenty-one to the spiritual world. Not only does this help us understand the Major Arcana, but it also helps us to understand holistic thinking by revealing how body, mind and spirit are connected along the spiritual journey.

Second Edition Author Note:

I used the term "holistic tarot" to discuss the idea that the Fool's Journey takes us through lessons that pertain to our care of body, mind and spirit. This was before Benebell Wen published her massive groundbreaking book by the same name. No correlation, other than that Benebell and I occasionally feel similarly about the cards, should be inferred.

* * *

Body: The Material World

Although the first seven numbered cards of the Major Arcana can all be interpreted as spiritual lessons, they can also be interpreted as components of our mundane lives. The Magician and the High Priestess can signify school and study, the Empress and Emperor can signify parenthood and adult responsibility, and the Emperor and Hierophant can signify our careers. The Lovers can denote our relationships, and the Chariot our transportation. On a deeper level, but still related to the material world, the Magician can signify outer personal identity and the High Priestess can signify inner personal identity. The Empress is the authority of the home, the Emperor is the authority of the community and the Hierophant is the authority of the church. The Lovers and the Chariot can each signify a different kind integration. The Lovers represents integration between personalities. The Chariot is integration between man and machine or man and his tools. This is particularly interesting since the Magician, back at the beginning of this cycle, is also related the use of tools. Clearly, being able to create, obtain and use tools is a basic skill that allows us to function in the material world.

There are many ways to look at these first seven cards, but we will always come back to the same idea. These cards each speak of the basic issues we all face in order to master the challenges of the material plane.

We begin our journey into the Material World with the Magician. Here, we understand that we, like the Magician, have all the tools we need. Our tools are in front of us. We make the commitment to learn to understand and use them. In life, those who learn to use their tools and develop skills have the most material success. The Magician symbolizes the commitment to that learning process.

The next card is the High Priestess. Here, having learned to use the tools around us, we now learn to use the tools within us. We patiently look within. We internalize our lessons and seek our own inner wisdom.

The Empress takes this wisdom and puts it in to action. With the Empress we manifest our skills, our tools, and our wisdom. It may be in the form of procreation or some other act of fertility or creativity. We learn to nurture our own needs and the needs of others. We create a home for our comfort and survival.

Having created a home with the Empress, we now create a community with the Emperor. We learn that our ability to be responsible and stable affects those beyond our four walls. We rule our own lives with wisdom and restraint and rise to create a governing force that extends beyond the home to the community at large.

After building community structures with the Emperor, we now create spiritual structures with the Hierophant. We understand the value of traditions and rituals within our society and within our own spiritual life. We accept our own authority and seek the teachings and authority of others when needed.

Having mastered external and internal learning with the Magician and the High Priestess, and the building of home, community and religion with the Empress, Emperor and Hierophant, we have now achieved the ability to make decisions, and to see both sides of a whole. In doing this, we come to understand our world and ourselves. We are now able to give and receive love as expressed in the Lovers.

Our final card in the journey of the Material World is the Chariot. Here, we experience mastery. We are in the driver's seat, in control of our own destiny, and able to move forward under our own power and will. In our current society, this energy is expressed by the young person who has done well in school, worked hard to earn both money and trust, and is now able to get a first driver's license and car.

Mind: The Emotional World

Many tarot decks begin the journey into the Emotional World with Strength. Others begin with Justice and visit Strength as the eleventh card. In this book we will address Strength as card eight and justice as card eleven. If you prefer it the other way you can certainly rewrite your journey into the emotional realm to reflect your preference.

The seven cards that denote the journey into the emotional world each deal with patience. To find emotional healing we must be patient with ourselves, patient with each other and patient with the process. Each card in this series also deals with control; either learning to maintain control of what we can, relinquishing the desire to control, or coming to terms with things that we do not control at all.

Acceptance is another theme of these seven cards. Each card reminds us of things that we must gracefully accept. Without acceptance, there is no emotional balance.

Strength, card eight, is all about being in control of one's more savage tendencies, so it is a good way to begin the journey toward emotional maturity. With Strength we learn that deep, abiding, patient love is more effective than anger, brute force, and physical strength. We learn to tame our own demons. At the same time, we learn to accept both the gentle and wild sides of our nature, and to use them in balance one with another.

In card nine, the Hermit, we learn the patience to seek wisdom when needed and to hold our tongues when our own wisdom is not requested. The Hermit holds the light of knowledge for all to see, but does not make an effort to share it unless it is sought. The Hermit also teaches us to be alone. We will never find our own emotional strength and healing in the company of others. Like the second card of the first journey, the High Priestess, we must look within ourselves. Fearless, quiet, meditative aloneness is required. The courage to accept, endure, and even enjoy our own company is a lesson of the Hermit.

In card ten we encounter the Wheel of Fortune. The Wheel teaches us to be secure in an insecure world. The Wheel reminds us that anything can happen, good or bad. The future is never set, never sure. There will always be ups and downs and unexpected turns. Our emotional health depends on our ability to understand this and anticipate it. One of my favorite images of this card comes from the *World Spirit Tarot*, which shows that we are all tied to a wheel that is turned by the Gods.

Justice, card eleven, is an answer to the inner child in each of us that screams, "That's not fair!" when we encounter life's ups and downs. It admonishes us to be fair with one another and to trust that the universe will balance everything out in the end.

Card twelve, The Hanged Man, tells us that when you can't change your situation, you must change your attitude. It reminds us not to struggle against our fate, but to accept the things we cannot control.

In card thirteen we accept complete change, whether we like it or not. The image of this card is usually scary, as is its name: Death. But on the path toward emotional healing we must be able to change, grieve, let go, and heal. The lessons that we have learned in cards eight though twelve each deal with a small piece of the greater whole that is card thirteen. All these cards help to prepare us for the ultimate transformation that we find in Death.

Card fourteen is the final card in our journey toward emotional balance and healing. Here, we find our balance, and the ability to blend together all the things life has to offer. We accept that nothing is perfect, but that we can become spiritual alchemists; to create our perfect blend. With Temperance, patience brings healing as we learn to manage our emotions.

Spirit: The Spiritual World

Every tarot card is spiritual. The Major Arcana contains the most spiritual cards of all. The last seven cards of the Major Arcana deal specifically with lessons learned as we focus on our spiritual growth. As we journey through the Major Arcana, the first series of seven Major Arcana cards teaches us to manage our physical lives and material resources. The second series of seven Major Arcana cards teaches us to manage and master our emotions. The final series of seven Major Arcana cards, cards fifteen through twenty-one, teaches us to find spiritual enlightenment.

The Devil begins that journey as he forces us to face our internal shadows and demons. With the Tower, we discover that enlightenment comes as we destroy those demons. The Star bathes us in heavenly light, while the Moon teaches us to look beyond that which we see with our eyes, discerning truth even when it is obscured by darkness. The Sun provides the courage to share our light with others. In Judgment, we find closure to the old and are born into the new. With the World, we have integration, attainment and completion.

We start our journey toward enlightenment squarely on Earth, not in heaven, face-to-face with our demons in card fifteen, The Devil. We face the chains that hold us down. We acknowledge the negative thoughts and habits that keep us from our growth.

The process of letting go may be an earth-shaking event. The Tower, in card sixteen, shows us that sometimes we must destroy our faulty foundations in order to rebuild a stronger structure. The destruction may be painful, but it is the only way to attain the freedom we seek.

After destruction comes healing, fulfillment, and satisfaction. In card seventeen, the Star, we drink in the abundance of life. Healing light and water surrounds us; our only challenge is to accept it.

Card eighteen shows us the deeper spiritual mysteries. We seek spiritual knowledge, but that which is seen by the light of the Moon can be unclear. Our intuition is the guide that shows us the hidden path.

Card nineteen, the Sun, teaches us to shine brilliantly. We are center stage and in control, our light is the brightest of all the lights in heaven. We have nothing to hide, and nothing to fear.

Card twenty, Judgment, shows us the end of all things. We learn to put closure to that which is behind us and are spiritually reborn.

Card twenty-one, The World, is the completion of the cycle. The world is ours. We have attained the enlightenment that we sought. We end our spiritual journey not in heaven, but right where we started, on Earth. The final lesson of enlightenment is the same lesson as the first told to us at the beginning of the Major Arcana. With the World, as with the Magician, we have everything that we need right in front of us.

Body, Mind and Spirit Exercises

Because tarot cards are numbered, it is easy to imagine that we travel through the Major Arcana and experience the lesson of each card in order. Often in life, our lessons don't happen in logical progressive order. We experience lessons of body, mind and spirit simultaneously. Often, we are more advanced in one area than another. Sometimes we learn the harder lessons first and must go back to learn the basics. We've all known people who can have out-of-body experiences at will but can't balance their checkbook!

Here is an exercise to help you ascertain your current lessons on your journey toward material, emotional and spiritual growth.

Look at cards one through seven and choose the one that you think most accurately represents where you are in your journey through the material world.

Now shuffle all seven cards, including the one that you just chose, and at random pick one to answer the same question. How does this card compare to the one you cognitively chose?

Now do the same exercise using cards eight through fourteen to describe your current place in your journey through the emotional world.

Finally, use the same exercise to describe your current position in your spiritual journey by using cards fifteen through twenty-one.

CHAPTER SIX

Reading Tarot

There are many ways to interpret the seventy-eight cards of the tarot and many ways to learn tarot interpretations. There are classes, books and websites to teach you methods of tarot interpretation. Some of your greatest discoveries will come from your own practice. By reading for yourself and others, and by keeping a tarot journal, you will learn how the cards speak to you.

There are a few things to keep in mind as you learn to read the cards. It is important to develop a list of keywords for each card. Use your tarot journal and include words that are traditional – the ones you learn from books, teachers and websites, even if they don't make sense to you. Add to that list the key words that really resonate with you, whether or not they are accepted as common key words for that particular card. Your list of keywords is dynamic and will grow over time. Even when you are a very experienced reader, your understanding of the cards will continue to change and grow. Your list of key words is personal. Even though it is important to understand traditional card meanings, you need to develop your unique relationship with the cards.

Each time you perform a reading, you will find new ways the cards speak to you and new ways the cards work together. With tarot the possibilities are limitless.

Divinatory meanings for all tarot cards can include the prediction of mundane occurrences such as travel or purchases. They can describe ideas, feelings or attitudes such as frustration, anger or inner peace. They can also give advice regarding spiritual challenges. They may suggest philosophies that need to be embraced or lessons that need to be learned. They can also represent specific people such as helpful people, those who bring us joy, or those who are having trouble or causing trouble.

More than one interpretation for a card may be simultaneously true within a reading. Some interpretations are more predictive, while others are contemplative. Some may refer to mundane activities, while others offer suggestions for spiritual growth.

Reversals

Many tarot traditions suggest that cards have a different interpretation when they are pulled upside down (reversed). Other traditions do not interpret the reversals. It is up to each reader to decide if they wish to honor reversals. Some common misconceptions about reversals include the idea that reversals are always negative or that reversals are always the opposite of the upright meaning of the card.

I think the best way to think about reversals is that when the card is reversed, the energy changes. It may indicate a delay or a lessening. It may suggest that the action the card would indicate would be inadvisable. It may add the word "no" or the prefix "un" to the key word associated with the card. It may suggest that the action or energy of the card was in the past.

Another way to think about reversals is to literally look at the card upside down, see what it does to the picture, and see what that looks like to you. For instance, when you hold the Three of Swords upside down, the swords can easily fall out of the heart. When you hold a Knight upside down, he has no way of moving forward.

As you think about reversals, make lists of keywords that you associate with each reversed card and memorize them along with your keywords for upright cards. This will give you a greater tarot vocabulary and will give more detail to your readings.

Intuitive Reading

Sometimes your focus will be drawn to a particular image within a tarot card, such as the bird or the snail in the Nine of Pentacles or the flower the Fool holds. No matter how minute the image is in contrast with the greater whole, the fact that your attention is drawn to it is significant. Whatever you see in the tarot image, or any part of an image, could be important to the reading.

Allowing yourself to be guided by the images and your feelings about them is part of intuitive tarot reading. Other aspects of intuitive reading include being open to any thoughts or ideas that come to you in the process of laying out, looking at and talking about the cards.

Second Edition Author Note:

While the practices of checking in with your thoughts and feelings during a reading, and of allowing your intuition to guide your visual focus on the cards are both important intuitive reading skills, there are many other ways to bring intuition into your readings. Intuition can guide your interpretation of the cards, and the wording you choose. Your intuition will help you know if the Page that appears, for example, is your child, your cat, your education, your need to communicate, or some combination of the above. In some readings your intuition may supply you with an unusual-but-accurate interpretation of a card.

Your intuition may also guide you to ask certain questions of the cards. When reading for others, your intuition may help you get to the root of your clients' concerns, even when your client is not terribly receptive.

※ ※ ※

The best tarot readings incorporate discussion of the images, the intuition of the reader, and traditional interpretations of the cards.

Spreads, Questions and Dialogues

Each tarot reader has a unique style of reading. There is no right or wrong way to ask questions and lay out cards. There are many ways to divine with tarot cards. Three popular ways are spreads, questions, and dialogues. We will explore each in this chapter.

Tarot spreads involve laying out the cards in a specific pattern. Each position usually has a meaning, although sometimes cards in specific positions are designated to be blended together and read as a group. Spreads can have just two cards, or many more. Spreads of three cards are popular and traditional.

Tarot spreads can be performed to answer a specific question or to give insight into a specific situation. Spreads can be performed to give a general overview and provide whatever information is most important.

Tarot questions allow the querent to ask a specific question. The reader pulls just one card, or sometimes a few cards, to answer the question. For instance, if the querent asks "will I be hired for the job I interviewed for today?" and you pull at random the Three of Pentacles, the answer is very likely yes. If you pull a card that does not seem to give a specific answer to the question, pull another card or two to give more information before you interpret the answer. Each card is pertinent, but sometimes it takes blending a few to get a full answer.

In a tarot dialogue, the answer derived from the card or cards stimulates another question, and so more cards are pulled. The question and answer dialogue can continue for as long as it needs to.

Never be afraid to experiment with the cards and find the ways that they work best for you.

Tarot Spreads

A tarot spread is a specific pattern for laying out the cards. While a spread can utilize any number of cards, most spreads have at least three cards, and fewer than fourteen. Most spreads designate a meaning for each position. As the card falls into a position, the position modifies its meaning. For instance, if the position is "Recent Past" and the card placed there is the Three of Swords, you can be very sure the querent has recently suffered a heartache, loss, or betrayal. If instead, the Three of Swords were in a "near future" position, you might assume the heartache has not happened yet, or that the querent is making decisions currently that could lead to such difficulty.

Tarot spreads can give a lot of information in a single reading. Cards laid out in a spread work together to form cohesive statements and themes. It is possible to find trends in card distribution and card combinations that strengthen meanings and give added information.

There are a few basic kinds of spreads. Predictive spreads speak of events in the past, present and future, and show a "timeline" of events. The Celtic Cross and The Seven Sisters are good examples of this kind of spread. Find both spreads at the end of this chapter.

Meditative or reflective spreads focus on the thoughts, feelings and, attitudes of the querent. There are no positions which predict the future. The Body, Mind and Spirit spread is a meditative, or reflective spread, and a great example of a three-card spread.

To try it, simply lay out three cards, one for Body, one for Mind, and one for Spirit. Interpret the Body card to refer to your health, how you may be feeling about or relating to your body. It could or even be a comment on how you are taking care of your body.

Interpret the Mind card to discuss your thoughts and feelings, what's on your mind, or how you are thinking or feeling about life. It may even be a comment on how you are nurturing your intellect, or your emotional life.

The Spirit card discusses how you are nurturing your spiritual life, and how you are experiencing your connection to Spirit.

While the Body, Mind and Spirit Spread is a meditative or reflective spread, it is true that certain cards might be interpreted to predict events of the future, even though that is not the goal or purpose of the spread. For example, if a person is calm and happy but the Five of Swords appears in the "Mind" position, you might predict that the querent will soon experience internal conflict.

Situational spreads may be predictive, meditative, or both. These are spreads designed to solve a specific problem, such as a decision-making spread or a love relationship spread.

Some tarot spreads are traditional, like the Celtic Cross, Tree of Life, or Zodiac spreads. In recent years, modern tarotists have designed many interesting and helpful spreads. Many new tarot books offer a selection of spreads, and advice about designing spreads. Some original spreads appear at the end of this chapter.

Tarot readers should feel free to design their own spreads for repeated use, or to use just once to handle a specific question or situation.

Asking Questions in a Reading

Some readers prefer a question or specific focus prior to laying out the cards in a spread. Other readers prefer to start by laying out the cards and see which questions or themes reveal themselves. Sometimes the cards that appear clearly show the problems and their obvious questions. Subsequent cards may need to be pulled, or further spreads might need to be done to give information on how the problems should be solved.

Whether you entertain questions at the beginning, middle, or end of a tarot reading, tarot readings always involve the answering of questions. Arguably, even a general reading starts with an inherent question such as "what's going on right now?" or "what does the universe want me to know right now?"

Whenever we ask questions of the tarot, it is important to remember the adage: "nonsense in, nonsense out." In other words, the quality of the question we ask directly determines the quality of the answer we receive.

What makes a quality question? First, the question should be based on something true. If I have no vocal talent but if I ask about my singing career, it's likely I will get cards that could be interpreted as "what career?" If instead I ask how I could best honor my desire to create music, I would likely receive an answer that would provide helpful information.

Second, the question should be as open-ended as possible. This gives the universe more room to work on our behalf. "Will I get the job I just applied for?" is a type of question that most people want to ask. A better question, though, is "what do I need to know about the job I just applied for?"

This is true for two reasons. It is not always easy to derive simply yes/no answers from tarot. Tarot speaks in nuances and subtleties and often wants to give much more information than a simple yes or no. And, since tarot wants to give a full picture, we should ask questions that allow that picture to develop. Perhaps you will be hired by the company you interviewed with, but for a different job than you expected. Perhaps there will be a hiring freeze, but you will be called back in many months.

Basically, if the most likely outcome is simple, the cards will give an obvious yes or no answer. But if the situation is likely to be more complex, the tarot reader needs to move past the yes or no questions to reveal the likely complications.

The second reason is this. What if you have applied for a job that will turn out to be a poor fit for you? Tarot has the ability to advise against something that you may think you actually want. It may even be able to tell you what the problems are likely to be. Tarot will give more of those helpful details when you ask broader questions.

Most questions can be broken into a series of questions. You may start with a yes or no question, and then ask further questions which will provide information that is more helpful.

Questions are best when they offer the opportunity to be proactive. "What do I need to do?" "What should my attitude be?" "What will be most helpful to me?" These are all better questions than something that gives a closed or yes/no answer like "Will this happen?" "What can I do to become successful?" is much better than "will I be successful?" because it allows the tarot to give you the tools you need, rather than a simple yes or no reply.

Taking time to devise the most helpful questions will always lead to the most helpful answers. Asking as many questions as you need to will always give the most complete answers.

Second Edition Author Note:

I've recently noticed that many readers limit the number of questions they ask. Some seem to think that a reading must focus on only one question. Some pro readers limit questions by charging per question. I firmly believe that the more questions asked in a tarot session the more helpful the session will be.

* * *

Tarot Dialogues

Asking questions of tarot will often lead to the natural process of dialoguing with the cards. A tarot dialogue is exactly as it sounds. Ask a question, pull a few cards to receive the answer, then formulate another question, and pull more cards. Continue this until you have clarity, and your questions are answered. A tarot dialogue can be a reading in and of itself, or it can be performed after a formal spread has been interpreted. A dialogue can be performed for a querent, or as part of a self-reading process.

I find it is best to pull whatever number of cards feels right, be it one, two, three, or more. I like to shuffle the cards back in to the full deck after each question. That way cards can repeat. Often, receiving the same card multiple times can be a very powerful message.

Create your Own Spreads

You can create a custom spread to handle a specific situation. You can also create a spread to use regularly over time.

To create a spread, first decide on the purpose of your spread, and then its name. Decide how many card positions you want, what each card position will mean, and how you will lay them out graphically.

You can be as innovative as you want. You can create a spread themed for a specific deck, such as a "Will of the Goddess" spread for a Goddess tarot. You can modify a traditional spread, such as the Seven Sisters, and make it your own.

You could decide, in advance, that there will be specific auspicious cards. For instance, it might be especially meaningful if the Fool falls into the significator position or if a Cups card falls into a "Water" position in a four elements themed spread.

You could base your spread on an upcoming holiday and arrange the cards in the shape of a holiday symbol, like a Christmas tree or a maypole. You could also have card positions that are associated with a list, such as a card for each of the four elements, or a card for each month of the year, each Pagan holiday, or each of the Twelve Steps.

You might design a spread to solve a specific problem. Sometimes designing a specific spread is an effective alternative to a tarot dialogue. You can create a position for each question, each option, and each significant person.

Tarot Spreads

Here are some tarot spreads for you to enjoy. Try them on yourself, and on friends and clients. Use your tarot journal to record your readings.

Feel free to modify these spreads as you wish, and to use these spreads as inspiration to create your own original spreads.

Celtic Cross

The Celtic Cross is the most traditional and most popular tarot spread of all time. Traditionally the Celtic Cross has ten positions. I use an eleven-card Celtic Cross. This is my usual spread for professional tarot readings. I included it in my first book, Fortune Stellar, as an example of a great professional tarot spread. I am including it here, as well, because it is an easy and comprehensive spread for beginners, professionals, self-reading, and reading for others. You can begin with a question or simply lay out to cards to get a general overview.

Figure 1 - Celtic Cross Spread

Card 1: Significator: Who the querent is at the present moment.

Card 2: Atmosphere: What surrounds the querent at the present moment.

Card 3: Challenge: What challenge the querent faces at the present moment.

Card 4: Foundation: What the querent brings to the present from the past.

Card 5: Past: The recent events of the querent's past.

Card 6: Crown: What is foremost on the querent's mind at present.

Card 7: Future: Likely events in the querent's future.

Card 8: People: Issues surrounding the querent's friends and family.

Card 9: Relationships: The querent's romantic life.

Card 10: Hopes and Fears: What the querent imagines, hopes for, and/or fears.

Card 11: Final Outcome: How this phase of the querent's life is likely to resolve.

Seven Sisters Spread

This is a short spread that functions very much like the Celtic Cross. It is a traditional spread and is sometimes called the Horseshoe Spread or the Rainbow Spread because of its shape.

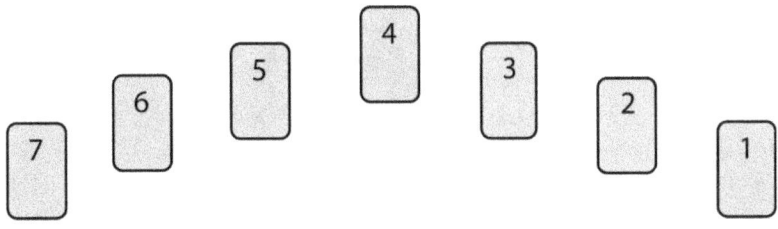

Figure 2 - Seven Sisters Spread

Card 1: Past: A significant influence, event, trait or value that happened or was formed in the past.

Card 2: Present: A current energy, event, concern or attitude in the querent's life at present.

Card 3: Future: A possible future event, or an ending to a current cycle or project. Something that is likely to occur in the near future.

Card 4: Significator: This card represents who the querent is at this current time, or in regard to the current question or situation.

Card 5: Close: A person or energy that is currently close to the querent, or in the querent's mind, at the current time.

Card 6: Challenge: The biggest problem, challenge or obstacle that the querent faces.

Card 7: Final Outcome: How this phase of the querent's life is likely to resolve.

Future Vision Spread

This is a complex and comprehensive predictive spread that I designed. Notice how it encourages the blending of card meanings and how cards can be interpreted in more than one way.

Tarot Tour Guide

When you interpret, first look for trends in suits and numbers. See how the cards work with each other.

Then, read the cards individually, with respect to their position.

Finally, consider the card formations.

Cards 1, 5 and 6 form a direct past, present, future reading.

Cards 1, 2 and 3 form a portrait of you.

Cards 3, 4 and 6 form your spiritual path.

Cards 1, 3 and 6 combine to determine what role, if any, fate or destiny plays in your desire to achieve this goal.

Figure 3 - Future Vision Spread

Card 1: Foundation Significator: What you bring from the past into the future. This is an unchanging aspect of you, a reference to who you are.

Card 2: Goal: What is it that you would like to do, or have happen, in the near future?

Card 3: Spiritual Help: How can you enlist spiritual energies to help you reach your goal?

Card 4: Challenge: Your biggest challenge or obstacle in achieving your goal.

Card 5: Your Assignment: The work you will need to do to reach your goal.

Card 6: Results: This will show your likely final outcome in regard to the goal you have set.

The Lamplighter Spread

I designed this meditative, or reflective, spread many years ago, inspired by a quote from Carl Jung.

> "One does not become enlightened by imagining figures of light, but by making darkness visible."

In the Lamplighter Spread each card represents a part of a lamp.

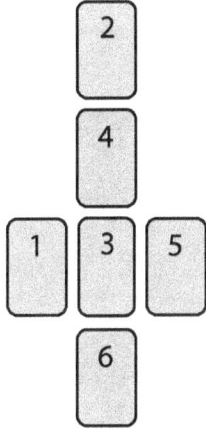

Figure 4 - The Lamplighter Spread

Card 1: The Darkness: What brings darkness, despair and misunderstanding to your life at this time?

Card 2: The Flame: What is the spark of hope and truth that will light your way and conquer darkness at this time?

Card 3: The Oil: What will fuel your flame and allow it to burn brightly?

Card 4: The Wick: What will be the path that brings the fuel to the flame?

Card 5: The Match: What will be your inspiration, a spark for your flame?

Card 6: The Lamp: What is the foundation for your flame, your light, and your hope? What supports it, holds it together and grounds it?

Mapping the Spiritual Path Spread

This is a spiritual situational spread. I designed it to help people understand their spiritual journey, and be proactive in their healing and growth.

Figure 5 - Mapping the Spiritual Path Spread

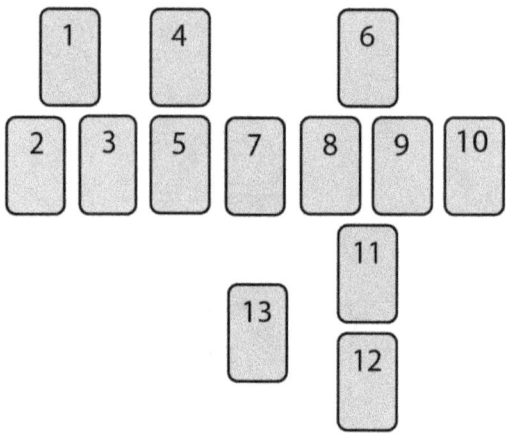

Card 1: What did I come here to learn?

Card 2: How do those lessons manifest in my life?

Card 3: What more must I do to learn those lessons?

Card 4: What do I want to learn?

Card 5: What must I do to learn this?

Card 6: What is the ultimate goal of my spiritual path?

Card 7: Actions to take supported by the element of Earth - Work and Stability.

Card 8: Actions to take supported by the element of Air - Personal Integrity.

Card 9: Actions to take supported by the element of Fire - Creativity and Growth.

Card 10: Actions to take supported by the element of Water – Emotions.

Card 11: What tools do I have to help me along my path?

Card 12: How do I unknowingly or unintentionally resist or sabotage my path?

Card 13: Where am I on my spiritual path right now?

Relationship Spread

This is a situational spread specifically for understanding relationships. You can use it for a love relationship, a familial or work relationship, or even to give insight into a potential future romance with someone you have yet to meet. Like most three-card readings, it is simply three cards in a row. Start by shuffling your deck. While you are shuffling, think about the relationship for which you are performing the reading.

After you shuffle, cut the deck into three piles. You will turn over and read the top card from each pile as follows.

The card furthest to the right represents the other person in the relationship. If you are reading for your own relationship, then obviously that is the person who isn't you. If you are reading for a querent, that is the person who isn't the querent. If you are reading about a relationship between two people you know, decide which person will be the card on the right, and which person will be the card on the left. If both people are present for the reading you can even have one person cut the deck to the left, and the other person cut the deck to the right.

When you turn this first card over, see how it describes the individual, and what they may be bringing to the relationship.

Now turn over the card on the left, leaving the middle card unrevealed. This left card will describe you, or your querent, and what you, or they, might be bringing to the relationship.

Now that cards to represent both people in the relationship are revealed, consider how these two cards fit together and what that says about the relationship.

When you are ready, turn over the middle card. This card describes the relationship itself at present.

Look at the three cards together and see what you can discern about the relationship.

If you need more information, you can "go deeper" by turning over the card, or even a few cards, from the top of each pile. You can see what is "underneath it all" by picking up the pile and looking at the very bottom card.

Exercise for the Advanced Student-Spreads

Create two new spreads in your tarot journal. Have the first be a predictive spread and the second a reflective/meditative spread. Perform both readings for yourself, one right after the other. How do the two readings compare, contrast and confirm each other?

CHAPTER SEVEN

The Four Elements: An Elemental Journey

As we have already discussed, the four elements are Earth, Air, Fire, and Water. Understanding the spiritual nature of the four elements helps us to understand tarot. Understanding the metaphysical properties of the four elements also helps us keep balance in our lives. Elemental thinking can be critical to magickal practice and personal healing.

We can describe the four elements as concepts, energies, or even spiritual entities. Many spiritual traditions across the globe honor the four elements. The four elements are summoned or invoked as entities or angels in magickal and spiritual practices from many cultures. Each tarot card correlates to one of the four elements.

An understanding of the four elements brings our material, spiritual, and emotional needs into focus and helps us to keep balance in our lives.

The element of Fire is associated with our passions, our desires, and our spiritual life force. Humor, creativity, sexuality and anger are all associated with Fire. The Major Arcana cards associated with the element of Fire are the Emperor, Strength, Wheel of Fortune, Temperance, the Tower, the Sun, and Judgment (please note that in some traditions Judgment is associated with Water instead of Fire). Fire is also associated with the Minor Arcana suit of Wands. The astrological signs of Aries, Leo and Sagittarius are Fire signs.

Water is the element associated with feelings, emotions, and matters of the heart. Water is the element of the tarot suit of Cups, and the Major Arcana cards the High Priestess, the Chariot, the Hanged

Man, Death, and the Moon. The astrological signs of Cancer, Scorpio and Pisces are Water signs.

The element of Air is associated with the powers of the mind. Truth, thought, and communication all belong to the element of Air. The Major Arcana cards associated with the element of Air are the Fool, the Magician, the Lovers, Justice, and the Star.

The Minor Arcana suit associated with the element of Air is Swords. The astrological signs of Gemini, Libra, and Aquarius are Air signs.

Earth relates to all physical matters, including work, health, wealth, and material goods. Earth is associated with the Major Arcana cards the Empress, the Hierophant, the Hermit, the Devil, and the World. The suit of Pentacles is associated with the element of Earth. The astrological signs of Taurus, Virgo, and Capricorn are Earth signs.

Table 1 - Element of Fire Chart of Correspondences

Element of Fire Correspondences	
Gender:	Masculine
Tools:	Wand, Branch, Candle, Igneous Rock
Cardinal Direction:	South
Zodiac:	Aries, Leo, Sagittarius
Colors:	Red, Orange
Animals:	Reptiles, Insects, Lizards
Minor Arcana Suit:	Wands
Major Arcana Cards:	Emperor, Strength, Wheel of Fortune, Temperance, Tower, Sun, Judgment
Expression:	I Do
Attributes:	**Powers of Vitality:** Passion, Creativity, Life Force, Growth, Sexuality, Humor, Anger, Spirituality, Energy, Motivation

Table 2 - Element of Earth Chart of Correspondences

Element of Earth Correspondences	
Gender:	Feminine
Tools:	Pentacle, Brown or Green Stone, Leaf, Coin
Cardinal Direction:	North
Zodiac:	Taurus, Virgo, Capricorn
Colors:	Green, Brown
Animals:	Land Mammals
Minor Arcana Suit:	Pentacles
Major Arcana Cards:	Empress, Hierophant, Hermit, Devil, World
Expression:	I Am
Attributes:	**Material Resources:** Money, Wealth, Home, Physical Goods, Health, Practical Matters, Stability, Grounding, Solidity

Table 3 - Element of Air Chart of Correspondences

Element of Air Correspondences	
Gender:	Masculine
Tools:	Sword, Feather, Incense, Crystal
Cardinal Direction:	East
Zodiac:	Gemini, Libra, Aquarius
Colors:	White, Yellow
Animals:	Winged Creatures
Minor Arcana Suit:	Swords
Major Arcana Cards:	Fool, Magician, Lovers, Justice, Star
Expression:	I Think
Attributes:	**Powers of the Mind:** Thought, Honesty, Communication, Clarity, Logic, Intelligence, Discernment, Reason, Integrity, Curiosity

Table 4 - Element of Water Chart of Correspondences

Element of Water Correspondences	
Gender:	Feminine
Tools:	Cup, Seashell, Blue Stone
Cardinal Direction:	West
Zodiac:	Cancer, Scorpio, Pisces
Colors:	Blue, Purple
Animals:	Water Creatures
Minor Arcana Suit:	Cups
Major Arcana Cards:	High Priestess, Chariot, Hanged Man, Death, Moon
Expression:	I Feel
Attributes:	**Matters of the Heart:** Emotion, Love, Compassion, Feelings, Intuition, Fluidity, Flow, Relationships, Family

As part of our spiritual journey it is important to understand how each element affects us and how each element works in our lives. The astrological circumstances of our birth give us natural elemental tendencies that we can be aware of but cannot change. Tarot is a wonderful tool to help us take control and bring balance to the elemental forces in our lives. With it we can discover which elemental energy may be lacking in our lives or which elemental energy is overly abundant.

For instance, the element of Fire brings passion to our lives. But people who have a great deal of Fire energy may be overly ruled by their passions. People who have too little Fire may have a hard time getting excited about anything.

Water allows us to feel our emotions. But if we have too much Water energy around us, we may become too focused on our own emotions. Too little and we may lack the ability to feel at all.

Air gives us clear thought and reason. But those with a great deal of Air energy may be overly analytical or may lack grounding. People who lack Air energy may have a hard time realizing or communicating their truths.

Earth gives us grounding, the ability to generate abundance and to stay on task. Too much Earth might stifle imagination or the ability to play and relax. Too little Earth may cause poverty, laziness, or a misunderstanding of reality.

Tarot allows us to get a feel for our current elemental balance. Whenever you spread the cards, take account of which elements are represented. Are they all there, in balance? Is there one that is missing? Is there one that is strongly prevalent? If you see that the elements are not in balance in a spread, try to figure out why. It may simply relate to things going on in your life. Or, it could be a sign that you are seriously out of balance; nurturing one aspect of life at the expense of another. For instance, if you were looking for a new job, lots of Pentacles would simply indicate the current focus. But if there were no obvious reason for the prevalence, the strong showing of Pentacles might suggest that you are too focused on money, too rigid in your routines, or needing to nurture more fun and imagination in your life.

Some tarot readers also employ elemental dignities in their tarot interpretations. Elemental dignities work on the idea that some combinations of elements are friendly, and others are enemies. When friendly elements come up together, they strengthen each other. When enemy elements come up together, they weaken each other. In this system, elements are always friendly with themselves. Fire and Air are friends, and Fire and Earth are friends. Water and Air are friends, and Water and Earth are friends. Fire and Water are enemies, and Earth and Air are enemies.

Whether or not you choose to study or use Elemental Dignities, it is interesting to think about how the elements might strengthen or weaken each other. For instance, we know that on a physical level, Air and Fire are friends because oxygen a feeds Fire. Think about what that means in a metaphysical sense. Air, which represents our thoughts, feeds Fire, which represents our creativity. It makes sense that contemplating a creative project will in fact enhance the project.

It is easy to see how Water and Fire are enemies on a physical level. On a metaphysical level, our emotional state (Water) can certainly affect our passions and creativity (Fire).

Earth and Air are more subtle enemies, in that they don't seem to affect each other on a physical level. But on a metaphysical level they are opposites: Air is expansive, curious and intelligent, while Earth is grounded, protected and stubborn.

None of the elements is 'bad' or 'good'. They are all necessary, each in balance. If you are interested in discovering your current elemental balance, you can do specific readings around that issue. You may simply ask which element is strongest in your life currently and pull a card. The element of the card would answer your question, and the meaning of the card itself might give you some insight as to how or why that element is working in your life. You could do the same thing in reverse by asking which element is least strong in your life currently.

Here is a sample reading using that method. On 1/2/05, I asked: "Which element is strongest in my life right now?" The card I pulled was The Moon Reversed. Since the Moon is a Water card, I took it to mean that Water is the element I am nurturing most strongly at present. Because the Moon is reversed, I took it to mean that perhaps I am putting too much emphasis on emotion to the detriment of my own balance. I attributed this to my Mother's untimely passing just a few months prior. I read the Moon reversed as saying, "There really is no mystery here, and of course your emotions will be out of whack while you are grieving." However, I also took the Moon reversed to say, "The death of my mother has caused me to question my faith in the spiritual wisdom that controls the mystery of life and death. To find emotional balance, and balance within the elements, I must trust the spiritual mysteries, even when I don't like what has happened."

Many readers have designed Elemental Balance Spreads. Here is one that I designed and enjoy using. You may use this as it is or create your own spread to help you determine elemental balance.

Compass Rose Spread for Elemental Balance

This spread gives information about your elemental balance, how it is affecting your life and what you can do about it! Interpret the cards as you normally would in any spread, but also pay close attention to the elements of cards 2 through 9 as they relate to their positions.

Write down the cards that appear in each position, interpret them, and spend some time in thought and meditation about them.

Figure 6 - Compass Rose Spread

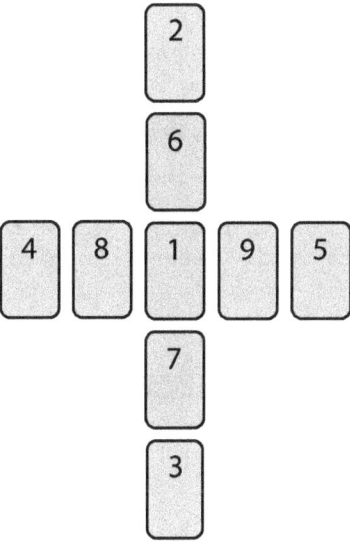

Card 1: Significator: This card describes who you are at the present moment. If the card belongs to the same element as your astrological birth sign it is particularly auspicious.

Card 2: Earth in the North: This card describes your current material and physical well-being. An Earth card here is extremely positive. If it is not an Earth card, take notice of which element it is. Perhaps that element is getting in the way of your best success at Earth matters. For instance, a Water card here might suggest that your emotions are getting in the way of your material success.

Card 3: Fire in the South: This card describes your life force energy, your creativity, and your passion for life. A Fire card here is a good sign. Any other element may be blocking your passion and creativity. For instance, and Earth card here may suggest that you need to relax and play.

Card 4: Water in the West: This card describes your emotional state. A Water card is preferred in this position. Another element in this position will give information about what is blocking or controlling your emotions. For instance, an Air card in this position may suggest that you are intellectualizing your emotions overly much.

Card 5: Air in the East: This card describes your state of mind. An Air card is most auspicious in this position. Another element may suggest what is controlling your thoughts. A Water card may suggest that emotions are getting in the way of your rational thought.

Look at cards 2,3,4,5. Is there one that stands out, or is stronger than the others? Or, does one strongly relate to Card 1, the Significator? In either case, that may be a prevalent element that could be helping or hurting you.

As you read the next four cards, continue to pay attention to the elemental correspondences of each card in conjunction with their positions.

Card Six: Earth Helpers: This is what is bringing you the best part of Earth or what can hurt or help you nurture Earth in your life.

Card Seven: Fire Helpers: This is what is bringing you the best part of Fire or what can hurt or help you nurture Fire in your life.

Card Eight: Water Helpers: This is what is bringing you the best part of Water or what can hurt or help you nurture Water in your life.

Card Nine: Air Helpers: This is what is bringing you the best part of Air or what can hurt or help you nurture Air in your life.

Restoring Elemental Balance

There are several ways to restore elemental balance in your life. Some are physical, some are meditative, and some involve tarot. Here is a tarot magick exercise you can use to restore your elemental balance.

The Compass Rose Spread for Elemental Balance can help you create better elemental balance in your life. Rather than laying out the cards at random, choose specific cards to put in each position that reflect the balance and energy you would like to see in your current life.

For instance, you may place the ace of each suit in its proper directional position. For helpers you may choose knights or pages or cards that represent help that you are trying to draw from within yourself or from around you. For the significator, choose the card that best represents the way you would like to see yourself and have it be a card that corresponds with the element of your own birth sign. You may surround this layout with any number of cards that symbolize the things you would like to be doing, thinking, and feeling at this time.

Once you have laid the spread, simply spend some time meditating with it. Perhaps you can leave it laid out on your altar overnight. Strengthen it by burning candles and incense, or by placing crystals around it.

There are simple meditations that can help you achieve better elemental balance. The technique is to visualize yourself in contact with the element that you need, or with all four elements at once. For instance, for Fire, visualize yourself sleeping on a beach in the sun or dancing around a campfire. For Water, visualize yourself swimming with dolphins or standing under a gentle rain or waterfall. For Air, visualize yourself flying or standing on a cliff facing the wind. For Earth, visualize yourself in a comfortable cave or walking in the woods. If you would like to try a more in-depth meditation, try the following meditation by having someone read it for you or by recording it for yourself.

Four Elements Meditation

Visualize yourself walking on a path through the woods on a bright, afternoon. There are leaves on the trees and the sun shines through them. A gentle breeze stirs the leaves, and the temperature is comfortable. Breathe in and smell the damp, living smells of the woods. Look around, and see ferns, wildflowers, trees, rocks, perhaps the occasional woodland creature, such as a rabbit or a squirrel. Look at your feet, and see the path made of leaves, small stones, and earth. You walk with a purpose, knowing that you have a destination. But you walk without fear, enjoying the afternoon in the forest.

Soon the path begins to get wider, and you know that you are coming to your destination. You are excited, but you consciously slow your breathe, and resist the urge to run forward. You continue to walk, and you see that your path leads to a large circular clearing in the woods, from which four more paths emanate. This clearing is covered in soft grass and offers a clear few of the blue sky. The paths are evenly spaced around the circle, one on which you have arrived, and four more. You know that today you will need to travel down all four of these paths.

You pick your first path and begin to walk on it. At first, it seems very much like the path that brought you here. But soon you realize you are walking uphill. The path becomes steeper, and you begin to breathe deeply as you climb. Soon, though, the path widens and flattens out, and you walk forward to see that you have come to a clearing, at the end of which is a cliff. You look out over the cliff and feel that you can see the whole Earth, and the whole sky. The breeze here is quite stiff, but not uncomfortable. You feel it most as you stand at the edge of the cliff without fear, and look around. You see birds in the sky, and for once, you do not envy their freedom, for you feel at this moment as free as the birds. You take a deep breath, and let the air fill your lungs. As you do, you feel mentally sharp. Everything that you see, you see with acuity and brilliance. You feel that you understand truth, that you are able to communicate your thoughts without hesitation.

You have come to the place of Air.

Now, you realize that on this cliff of Air there is a temple just for you. This is a place where you can come to clear your mind, to think, to understand, to formulate your words, and to heal from the harsh words of others. To find your temple you close your eyes. The breeze has turned to a strong wind, and blows against you, as you turn around in a circle three times. When you open your eyes, you are standing in front of your temple of Air.

What does it look like? What is it made of? Does it have a door, or is it open to the outside? Does it have walls and ceilings, or simply the sky around you? Are there tools here, tools of the magical or the mundane, which will help bring the Air energy to you? You take a moment to look around, walk around, see and experience your temple, all that it is, and all that it contains.

Now, you stand in your temple and breathe, feeling the peace of clarity and integrity flowing into your mind and body.

You commit the features of your temple to memory and know that you will return here, whenever you have the need.

Your journey for the afternoon is far from over, so you know that you must be going. Before you leave, you take one thing from the temple, a tool, a memento, something that will help you conjure the energy of Air when you need it and guide you back to your temple of Air.

What is it that you have taken?

Now, you walk back down the steep hill, down the path, and return to the clearing of five paths.

You choose a second path and begin the next part of your journey.

This path is narrower, and the air is a little chillier, although the sun is still bright. You walk down the path, and as you do you feel more and more excited. Your heart is like a drumbeat, urging you onward. Finally, you come to a large circle of tall trees. In the center is a huge stone ring. Inside that is a fire. The fire burns and crackles, and the flames rise high. No one seems to be tending it, yet it is both fed and controlled. It is brilliant, the flames dance in many colors, and in them you see pictures—things that have been, things that are, and things that might be. In your mind you hear music, and in your body you feel a limitless supply of energy.

Here is the place of Fire.

In this place of stone and flame you feel creative, able, and passion for your life. All that you have wanted to accomplish is within your grasp. You know, too, that there is a Fire temple here that is all yours, a place that you can return to for inspiration and energy.

As you close your eyes, the flames grow higher and hotter. You turn around three times and open your eyes. You are standing in front of your temple.

What do you see? What is your temple made of? What colors do you see? Are there items present, tools of creativity, things that inspire? You take a moment to look around, walk around, see and experience your temple, all that it is, and all that it contains.

Now, you stand in your temple and breathe, feeling the excitement of creation and inspiration burning in your mind and body.

You commit the features of your temple to memory, and know that you will return here, whenever you have the need.

Your journey for the afternoon is still not over, so you know that you must be going. Before you leave, you take one thing from the temple, a tool, a memento, something that will help you conjure the energy of Fire when you need it, and guide you back to your temple of Fire.

What is it that you have taken?

Now, you walk back down the narrow path, and return to the clearing of five paths.

You choose a third path and begin the next part of your journey.

The path that you choose this time is smooth, and as you look down you see that the earth is replaced by sand. Instead of woodland ferns you see grasses, waving in the gentle breeze. Smooth stones and seashells begin to appear. As you inhale, you smell salt in the air.

You continue walking and see that your sand path is becoming a sandy beach. You can't yet see the shoreline, but you see the blue horizon where the water meets the sky, and you hear the surf against the shore and smell the salt air.

You walk, all the way down to the shore and see the great expanse of water, rising and falling with the waves. You feel the sand on your feel, and then the waves, pulling gently, rushing up to greet you and then falling back.

You have come to the place of Water.

The ocean rises to cleanse you soul of sadness, to heal your emotional hurts. In this place of Water you are renewed and refreshed. Your heart is healed, and you understand compassion, and the mysteries of love. There is a temple of Water here for you. To find it, you close your eyes. You hear and feel the waves rising, pounding against the sand as you turn, three times, and open your eyes to find you temple.

What does it look like? What is it made of? Are there items present, tools of cleansing, things that make you feel loved? You take a moment to look around, walk around, see and experience your temple, all that it is, and all that it contains.

Now, you stand in your temple and breathe, feeling the soothing and cleansing of emotional purity and the depth of unconditional love in your heart.

You commit the features of your temple to memory, and know that you will return here, whenever you have the need.

You still have one more place to visit today, so you know that you must be going. Before you leave, you take one thing from the temple, a tool, a memento, something that will help you conjure the energy of Water when you need it and guide you back to your temple of Water.

What is it that you have taken?

Now, you walk back down the sandy path, and return to the clearing of five paths.

You begin your journey down the last path.

On this path, you see that there are many trees, of many varieties. The earth is rich beneath your feet, and you see flowers blooming from the ground. There are fruits hanging from many of the trees. As you look through the trees into the forest, you see all manner of woodland animals. There are deer, watching you as you watch them.

You walk for a while along the path, marveling at the many kinds of plants and animals that you see. You come to a place, not really a clearing this time, but a wide spot in the path. The path is running along a mountain side, and in the side of the mountain, at the wide spot in the path is a door that seems to go right into the mountain. As you look around, you can see that the side of the mountain is planted with gardens. A waterfall tumbles into a stream. You see that every manner of food, shelter, and comfort is available to you, and you feel safe and secure. You have come to the place of Earth.

This is the place where you can feel grounded, safe, and at home. It is a place of physical healing, security and abundance, a place of health and wealth. It is time to discover your temple of Earth. You walk up to the door in the mountainside and reach your hand for the doorknob. You close your eyes and count to three. When you open your eyes, the door is opened, and you are within your temple.

What is your temple of Earth, and what is here to make you comfortable? What does it look like, and what are you items available to you? Stand in your temple and breathe, breathing in the richness, the abundance, the bounty and security of the Earth.

You commit the features of your temple to memory, and know that you will return here, whenever you have the need.

Your journey today is nearly over. Before you leave, you take one thing from the temple, a tool, a memento, something that will help you conjure the energy of Earth when you need it and guide you back to your temple of Earth.

What is it that you have taken?

Now, you walk back down the fruitful path, and return to the clearing of five paths.

You stand in the clearing and take stock of the four items you have collected, one from each temple. These items will travel with you always. They will help you conjure the clarity of Air, the inspiration of Fire, the cleansing of Water and the abundance of Earth.

They will remind you to return to your temples to connect with the elements whenever you have the need.

Now, your journey is at an end. You have accomplished much. You begin your walk down the first path, the path the first brought you to this place, to return to the place where you started.

Summoning the Elements

When possible, it is good to connect with the four elements physically. For Fire, light candles, have a fire in the fireplace or in a fire circle. For Water, go swimming or soak in a tub. For Air, fly a kite, go for a run, or blow soap bubbles. For Earth, walk in the woods, bake bread, or tend plants.

If we think of each element as a spiritual force, we understand that each element can be summoned or invoked. Once summoned, we can ask the element to bestow its energy to us. We might summon Earth if we need to feel more grounded or if we needed money. Water will bring emotional health. Fire can be summoned to stimulate creativity. We can summon Air to reveal truth or to facilitate clear thought.

There are many ways to invoke the elements. It can be done with thought, with spoken word or with song. There are symbols and tools that can be used to summon the elements. You may know that the traditional four tools of magick are the tarot Minor Arcana icons. The four tools of magick, like the suit icons, each correspond with an element, and a cardinal direction.

You can purchase or fashion a pentacle and place it on the north side of your tarot altar, or your room, to summon Earth. A cup in the west will summon Water. Use a wand in the south to summon Fire and a sword or knife in the east to summon Air.

Items from nature work well for the same purpose. For instance, a feather can represent Air, a shell can represent Water, igneous rock or a candle can represent Fire, and a stone can represent Earth.

Using tarot cards as the tools of the four elements works equally well. For instance, the four aces can represent the four elements.

Many Earth-based religions have prescribed rituals for invoking the elements to create sacred space or perform magick. Here is an invocation to the four elements (also known as a Call to the Quarters) that I wrote many years ago.

Call to the Quarters

Airs of East, alight, arise!
Kiss eagles' wings and touch the skies!
Your breath will to our magick bring
The power of mind within our ring.

Red flames of South leap round the ring
And to our magick Fire bring!
The salamander rises high,
Let passion flow from Earth to sky!

Beings of Water, swell the tide,
Bring westward dolphin to our side!
Lead us to the depths of love
As oceans swirl below, above!

Element of Earth draw near!
Bring buffalo spirit to us here.
Health, abundance, birth and death,
Earth Mother, hold us at your breast.

Most magickal teaching suggests that if you invoke the elements, you must also dismiss them at the end of your meditation, circle, divination or magick. Remember that any element out of balance or out of control may cause disturbances that are not only emotional or symbolic, but also physical and destructive. I remember being part of an informal circle that was interrupted while we were dismissing the Fire element. For days after, each person that had been in that circle noticed they received minor inadvertent burns much more frequently than they would have expected.

To dismiss the elements, thank each in turn, and bid them farewell. You may request that each leave with you some of their attributes. For instance, you may ask Air to leave your clear thought, Fire to leave you inspiration, Water to leave you the ability to love, and Earth to leave you prosperity.

Here is rhyming dismissal that you may use if you prefer.

Dismissal to the Quarters

Airs of East and winds that blow
To your watchtower you must go
Thank you for your presence here
Leave us with thought and reason clear.

Red flames of South that glow and burn
To your watchtower now return
Thank you for your sparks so bright
That leave our hearts and minds alight.

Beings of Water, Westward tide,
To your watchtower now abide
Leave us all your depths of love
As oceans swirl below, above!

Return Earth to Northward tower
Thank you for your strength and power
Leave us hope and leave us health
Bless our hearths, our homes, our wealth.

Through tarot divination and magick, through invocation and meditation and through physical, symbolic and spiritual connection, we are able to find elemental balance in our lives.

Through understanding the elements and their influences, we develop greater understanding of ourselves, and of our spiritual journey. As we see the correlations between the four elements and tarot, we develop a fuller understanding of tarot.

Correlations are drawn between tarot and many occult systems. It is unclear to tarot historians if the original tarot developers intended these correlations, although there is no historical evidence they did. It is possible, and even likely, that the neat fit of tarot and astrology, or tarot and the Kabalistic Tree of Life, is simply a happy coincidence. It is also true that many tarotists believe that this happy coincidence is part of a greater spiritual design created not by humans, but by the very spirit or spirits who speak through the tarot.

It is not necessary to know and understand every occult system that correlates with the tarot in order to be a great tarot reader. It would be difficult to have a true understanding of tarot without understanding the four elements of life.

CHAPTER EIGHT

The Element of Air- Thinking, Learning, Communication, Integrity

The next four chapters focus on the four elements and their connections to tarot. We will begin with Air, and its influence on learning, interpreting, and reading tarot. Every student should understand each card and have a sense of how the tarot works for them. We can only gain such understanding through study, memorization, reading and writing. The study of tarot requires focus and clarity. To read for others required integrity and clear communication. That is why the first element that we will work with is the element of Air. We will follow with the element of Earth, where we will explore use of tarot in matters of practicality, resources and career. Then we will travel to Water and explore how tarot is used to deal with issues of love, relationships, fellowship and emotional balance and healing. Finally, we will look at Fire, and how tarot is used in creative and spiritual processes.

Because Air rules the mind, we will call on it to assist our tarot journey by bringing us the ability to study and focus, along with skills of memorization and communication.

Air is our intelligence and our integrity. Through Air we find focus, clarity and understanding. Air is the cleansing breath, the new outlook, and the original thought. Air rules all powers of the mind. It can bring logic and clarity; it can also bring worry and anxiety. Hurtful thoughts and words come from Air, as does the power to undo that hurt through clear thought and reason. Air commands truth, thought, and word. Air is clear understanding and the undeniable truth. Air is the single idea that gives rise to all of creation.

Invocation of the Air

The Ace of Swords is a magickal tool that invokes the Air. To study tarot, your mind must be sharp. To read tarot, your mind must be logical. To use the cards as tools of spiritual growth, you must first understand them intellectually.

Look at your Ace of Swords and see it as the core symbol of truth, thought and reason. Hold the Ace of Swords high above your head and take a deep breath. Be conscious of the air that you breathe in and know that it brings you clarity and understanding. Welcome Air into yourself, and say an invocation, such as the following.

"As I breathe in the Air of life, I bring Air to my spirit. With this sword I bring knowledge, understanding, clarity, and the power of mind to myself that I may use it in the study of tarot, to discern my spirit's path, and to be truthful and wise in all matters.

With this sword and my breath, I call the powers of Air. Let my mind be open. Let my wits be sharp. Let my words be true. May Air bring me understanding of spirit, understanding of tarot, and a clear vision for my journey."

Swords Air Exercise

Look at the Swords cards two through ten. Each of these cards represents a form of thought. As you look at each card, what mental process do you see in each one?

Choose the cards that represent the states of mind that will help you most in your tarot studies.

Now look at the cards you didn't choose. Do these cards represent ways of thinking that could impede your tarot journey?

Major Arcana Air Exercise

Place the Major Arcana cards that are traditionally associated with the element of Air in front of you. They are the Fool, the Magician, the Lovers, Justice and the Star.

Think about these cards in association with what you know about the element of Air.

How do each of these cards symbolize the element of Air?

What do you learn about Air when you look at these cards?

What do you learn about each of these cards when you think of it as a symbol of Air?

Clues for the Beginner -Air: The Study of Tarot

When you first begin to learn tarot, it is easy to be overwhelmed by all the information. Eventually, you will need to memorize all seventy-eight cards. For now, feel comfortable referring to books and notes when you do readings.

See if you can make sense of the cards that come up based on what you read about the cards and what you see in the card images. This is the first step of learning to read tarot. You will be surprised by the insightful readings you are able to give even before you have committed the cards to memory.

Tarot, Meditation and the Search for Clarity

One of the most sought-after gifts of Air is clarity. Meditation and tarot are partners in the search for clarity. We have already discussed the idea that tarot is a meditative tool. Tarot reading offers opportunity for reflection, and for conversation with the Universe. Tarot study offers the opportunity to contemplate universal themes and truths. Tarot can serve as an aid to meditation by offering an image or concept to contemplate, or inspiration for guided imagery. In turn, meditation can help us more deeply understand the tarot cards.

Many tarot students and readers pick one card at random every day as a focus for meditation. There are many ways to use a tarot card in meditation. One is to simply breathe and stare at the card and ask the card to tell you about itself. See what comes into your mind as you look at the card.

Another is to put yourself into the action of the card. Imagine a conversation with the card character. Let yourself sit in the throne of the High Priestess, for example, or step off a cliff like the Fool.

You can also write about the card and meditate on its meaning. You can let your vision go soft and focus on the patterns and colors of the image.

If you are having a problem or issue, look through your cards and choose one cognitively that speaks to your current issues. Then, meditate with it to gain clarity around your situation.

Many cultures use sacred pictures in prayer and meditation. Photographs of gurus, drawings of Jesus and Mary, statues of Goddesses and pictures of saints all serve not only as a reminder, but also an invocation of deity. Tarot cards are also sacred pictures, and can be used in prayer, meditation and invocation, just the same way other sacred pictures are.

Meditation Exercise

Think of a current problem or situation. Look through your cards, and cognitively choose one that presents an answer or resolution to your problem. Meditate with that card by looking at it and asking it what you can do to bring its energy into your life.

Reading for Yourself and Others

Important attributes of the element of Air are integrity, honesty, communication, clear and ethical intent, and carefully chosen words. These are also necessary qualities for a good tarot student and a good tarot reader.

Not every tarot student chooses to read for others. Some prefer to use the cards for their own reflection and for personal spiritual guidance.

Not every reader chooses to read professionally. Some prefer to read for family and friends, or to do it just for fun, or to donate their services to charities.

The rumor continues to circulate amongst new students that one should never try to read tarot for oneself. I believe that if one does not read for oneself, one should never attempt to read for others. I think the only way to know how the cards really speak to you is to use them frequently for yourself.

The obvious problem is that when you read for yourself (or for anyone you care about) you can't possibly be objective.

It is also possible to dissolve into a puddle of your own anxieties by obsessively pulling card after card to give you some predictive information, such as "is he going to call me?" or "will I get the job?" When we read for ourselves, we need to constantly remember that tarot's most helpful function is to provide spiritual wisdom and strategic advice, not to assuage our anxiety about a latest crush or exciting opportunity.

There is a different energy between reading for a stranger and reading for someone with whom you have a personal relationship. When we care about someone, we become attached to a desired outcome, or have our own strong ideas about what that person should do, or what we want to happen. There is always the temptation to use the cards to present our own opinions. And, when reading for ourselves or those close to us, our own desires for specific outcomes may make it hard to correctly interpret cards in a predictive way.

So, it may be true that it is easier to do a predictive reading for someone we've never met. But predictions are just a small part of what tarot reading should be. It's interesting, though, that a professional reader's ability to give accurate predications is often what causes their reputation to grow and their business to prosper.

Many readers discover that they are better at delivering some aspects of tarot readings than others or at making some types of predictions than others. It is good to know your strengths and weaknesses as a reader, just as it is good to know how the cards speak to you. But remember that you will always continue to grow as a reader. Your understanding of the cards will change and your ability to use your own gifts will change. It is important to be open to the changes that make you better at giving readings and at using the cards.

Whatever your best tarot skills are, to see the tarot only in terms of future predictions is not only very limiting, but also wrong.

Whether reading for yourself, your friends or strangers, use tarot first and foremost as a tool of spiritual guidance. Let the cards bring focus, wisdom and new ideas that will serve as a guiding light for whatever the future may bring.

Second Edition Author Note:

Is it possible to be objective when reading for oneself, or for someone one cares about? In re-reading this section I was surprised that I had flat-out written that one can't possibly be objective. As much as I appreciate the honesty of my younger self, these days I have a slightly different perspective.

Yes, it is hard to be completely objective when you care, but it's worth trying. The process of coming to a place of spiritual neutral, or compassionate detachment, is a valuable exercise, and one that can lead to some helpful divination.

***

Exercise: What is a Tarot Reading?

Let's use some "Air energy" to figure out all the things that a tarot reading can be. Here's my list, see what you can add to it!

A tarot reading can be fun and entertaining.

A tarot reading can give insight into your own personality and show how others perceive you.

A tarot reading can give advice about your relationships with other people.

A tarot reading can give you an idea of what you need to be learning or focusing on at present.

A tarot reading can predict possible future events.

A tarot reading can facilitate communication with the spirit world.

A tarot reading can provide insight, clarity and direction.

A tarot reading can explain past events and thereby help with the process of closure.

A tarot reading can offer new solutions to old problems.

A tarot reading can help you set goals for the future.

A tarot reading can help you assess your strengths and weaknesses.

A tarot reading can facilitate communication between people.

A tarot reading can help define your life's purpose.

A tarot reading can offer validation of feelings and ideas.

A tarot reading can help you access your higher consciousness, and the spirit guides around you.

Good News, Bad News

Many laypeople seem to fear tarot reading because they are afraid that they will "hear bad news." Likewise, some readers are afraid to give "bad news" and so they sugar-coat their readings, while other readers cavalierly give gloom-and-doom predictions without any concern for the damage they are doing.

Often in my career I have had to comfort clients who have received recent readings from other readers that gave very negative predictions. These clients want to see if I concur and to see if I can offer any solutions. Often, I just don't concur at all, although I may see the area of stress that the reader was referencing. For instance, one client was told that she and her husband would get divorced the following September. I saw no such thing, but I did see that there were problems in the household and offered some solutions for improving attitudes and communication.

I believe that a tarot reading should always be empowering. There is always something that a client can do to improve their situation in some way. It is the job of the reader to find and present that advice. Whether the client chooses to take that advice or not is not the readers' concern. Some readers become very frustrated with clients who ask for advice and don't follow it. It is important that neither a reading nor a reader interfere with a client's free will.

As for my client for whom a divorce was predicted, she and her husband are still happily married. However, they did do some major home renovations that September which caused stress and did, quite literally, tear their home apart. What a good example of how a misinterpretation of a card and a poorly delivered reading can cause pain and anxiety!

But what if, while reading for a client, you really do see a serious problem? It is very important to act within your ethics, and to be prepared for the situation so that when it happens you can do your best for the client.

In the very beginning of a reading you should quietly assess your client's willingness and ability to hear difficult news. In other words, how much can this person handle, and what do you think they would do with difficult information? Would they feel that "forewarned is forearmed," and be appreciative? Would they take steps to avert a problem? Or would they simply lose sleep and spend energy on stress and despair?

Whenever you make a future prediction, you need to ask yourself two questions before you speak. One is "What if I'm wrong?" The other is "What if I'm right?" You can even quietly pull some cards to give you, as the reader, advice on what to say and how to say it.

Because each card has so many possible meanings, sometimes it is helpful to give each possible meaning and let the client figure it out. Let's go back to my last example of the couple and their predicted divorce. Suppose one of the cards that gave the reader the idea of divorce was the Ten of Pentacles reversed. The reading would have been great, and no damage would have been done, if the reader had simply suggested that the card could mean a number of things. It could mean a problem in the marriage, a problem with money or real estate, or significant home repair. She might say "There is something in your home that needs repair. It may be your marriage, it may be finances, or it may be the home itself." From there, they could read on all the issues, without ever making an unfortunate or inaccurate prediction.

It is also important to give the news as you see it. I had another client who was very excited to tell me that she was expecting her first grandchild. She asked me about it, and what I saw. The cards that came up included the Three of Swords, and I strongly felt there would be a miscarriage in the first trimester. I looked further and pulled more cards. There were a few difficult cards, and then, finally, the Ten of Cups. I said, "I am so happy for you, but I want you to be aware that there is a possibility that this pregnancy will result in an early miscarriage. If that happens, it will be your job to help everyone be strong and get through it and have the courage to try again. I do see healthy grandchildren for you in the future, but perhaps not as quickly as you are now thinking."

The next time I saw this client she gave me a hug and thanked me for preparing her for the loss of the pregnancy. She was happy to report, though, that her daughter was once again expecting, and felt that the reading had put her in the position of helping her family look to the future instead of the past.

It is often true that when a difficult event is predicted and comes to pass, people have a sense of comfort in thinking that it was simply fate, something that was meant to be, and beyond their control.

I think in a case like this, and in most cases, what you say is important, but how you say it is even more important. Future predictions are possibilities, not certainties, and need to be presented as such. Before each reading, I say a prayer and call on the element of Air to give me clear vision and to give me the ability to speak in a way that is truthful, clear, compassionate and hopeful.

We have already said that the energy of reading for friends and family is different than the energy of reading for strangers. It is also true that if you read for the same client many times the energy of the readings will change because you have developed a more intimate relationship. To avoid that energetic change some readers refuse to read for someone more frequently than every six months.

I don't tend to refuse readings, and I enjoy seeing the client-reader relationship transform as I get to know the client and get to see the patterns that come up in the cards over time.

The advantage of reading for a regular client, or a friend or family member, is that you know their habits, their history and their goals, and you can point out their growth and the changes they embrace. You can see the seeds that were planted come to fruition. You will remember some of the cards that come up regularly for them and help them to see a deeper meaning in those cards.

Overall, my experience is that readings for people I know well tend to be more spiritual and strategic and more about tracking progress. Readings for people I don't know or see infrequently are more predictive and deal more with current issues and problems.

If reading for someone we know is different that reading for someone we don't know, then what is it really like to read for ourselves? I think we when approach reading for ourselves it should always be spiritual in nature and should always be about challenging ourselves to do our best, to grow and to learn.

Second Edition Author Note:

I realize that I've consistently made a distinction between 'spiritual' readings and 'predictive' readings and haven't clarified what that means. All readings can have spiritual components and predictive components. When I refer to these two foci as opposites of sorts, here's what I mean.

A spiritual reading, in this context, focuses on attitude, opportunity for growth, personal insight and messages from the Universe, and/or from loved ones in spirit. A spiritual reading finds meaning in heartbreak and encourages healing and positive thought. A spiritual reading offers the querent responsibility for their future.

Many times, this spiritual sort of reading does feel like the opposite of a sort of predictive reading where the querent wants simply to know what will happen and does not particularly want to take responsibility for making things happen. Very often these sorts of querents have a hard time believing that the future may be neither set nor predicable; that what we think, say and do can indeed shape our future.

***

As tarot students on a spiritual path, we must each decide the best way to use the cards for ourselves and for others. The rule that must be constant and consistent is that our use of the cards should never bring harm, either intentionally or inadvertently. We must be ever vigilant to make sure we are using the cards to bring insight, courage and growth rather than fear and anxiety, for ourselves and for others.

Tarot, Decisions and Attitudes

Tarot is a wonderful tool to assist in decision making. While we should never let the cards 'make a decision' for us or our clients, we can do a few things with the cards that are helpful in the decision-making process.

First, working with the cards will force us to clearly enumerate all our possible options. Then, we can discover if there are possibilities that we had not previously considered. Tarot can also help us to think about all the factors involved in choosing a path. With tarot, we can call on our higher selves, our spirit guides, our angels and our departed loved ones to weigh in on our choices. We can play 'what if' and look for likely outcomes for each path we may choose. We can meditate and do magick using cards that represent good decisions, positive outcomes, and decisive action to assist us.

Most people are uncomfortable making decisions. We worry that we will choose badly or that someone will not approve of our choices. Tarot is an impartial guide that will help us to have the focus, clarity, and courage we need.

When you need to make a decision, sit with your tarot journal and write down the options that you see for yourself. If you are working with a client who is seeking your help in decision-making, get them to clearly state the options as they see them.

Shuffle the deck as you ground yourself and say a prayer for clarity, understanding and a positive outcome. Think about each path in front of you and ask the question "Is there any other path or choice that I should be considering?" Pull a card. If the card seems to indicate a path, add that choice to your list. If the card doesn't make sense, pull a few more and look at them together. Do you see other options here? It may be that your estimation of your options was correct, or that the cards have helped you see new possibilities.

Now, pull one card for each possible path. Again, it is fine if you need more than one card. It is good to be intuitive about the number of cards you draw. Interpret these cards to give you an idea about what you might expect with each choice. Now, think about outcome. Shuffle all your cards again and pull one card to give you information about the ultimate best-case outcome that you desire. Put that card back and shuffle again. Pull cards for each path, this time thinking about what the ultimate outcome will be if you take each path. Compare these cards to the card you pulled to describe the best-case outcome. Compare all these cards to your own hopes and vision.

By now you should be seeing a clear trend toward one direction. If two different paths seem to have a similar outcome, you can ask if there are any factors you hadn't considered for either path and pull more cards. You can also ask what factors you should weigh most heavily when making your choice. You can ask how specific people might be affected by your decisions and pull some cards. You can ask the opinion of the spirits around you and pull some cards.

Write down or discuss all the information you receive and let it help you in your process.

If you need to meditate or do magick with the cards to help you find your clarity and courage to make a decision, try the Ace of Swords, the Knight of Swords, or the King of Swords. Each of these cards represents intelligence, clarity, courage, integrity, mental strength, and decisive action.

Cards that can represent the need for a decision are the Lovers, the Fool, and the Two of Swords. Justice, Judgment and the Two of Pentacles can also represent decisions, as can the Seven of Cups and the Four of Cups. Sometimes we don't even know we have choices or options in front of us, or the need to make an important decision, until it comes up in a reading!

Another mental process the tarot can help with is attitude adjustment. Often, we feel sorry for ourselves, or filled with fear and worry. Sometimes this is an appropriate part of a healing process. Other times, our attitudes aren't at all helpful and can be hard to shake!

There are many tarot cards that can speak of difficult attitudes. Both the Four and Five of Cups can discuss an attitude of pessimism. The Five of Pentacles can discuss a feeling of being left out. The Eight of Cups can discuss a feeling of abandonment. The Seven of Wands and the Nine of Wands can portray an attitude of defensiveness. The Eight of Swords discusses anxiety. The Nine of Swords can be real clinical depression, or it can be an attitude of sorrow or feeling sorry for oneself. The Four of Pentacles can discuss an attitude of either selfishness or impoverishment. Justice, when reversed, can reflect a feeling of being treated unfairly.

What do you say to someone whom you are reading for whose cards clearly display a bad attitude? What can you do to correct your own bad attitude?

There are a few cards that come up to offer suggestions. The Hanged Man says that if you can't change your situation, you'll have to change your attitude. Strength reminds us to balance our wild nature with a discipline of gentleness. The Wheel of Fortune reminds us that what goes around comes around in its own time. Justice tells us that justice will be served and eventually the scales will be balanced.

Often when we seem to need an attitude adjustment, the first things we really need is compassion, validation, and the ability to vent. As readers, we need to provide this to our clients. When reading for ourselves, we need to be able give these gifts to ourselves, or to seek a proper venue for them.

When we are upset about something that has happened, it is advisable to shuffle the deck and try to find a spiritual answer. "What is the greater purpose in this?" is a question you can ask. "What am I to learn from this?" is another. When reading for others, these are helpful questions that the client may not think to ask. If you provide both the question and the answer, you will be well on your way to providing the needed attitude overhaul.

When we are confronted with difficult situations, a great question to ask the cards is "What should be my attitude about this?" When we pull a card and are receptive to its answer, we can adjust our attitude. In turn, this changes the energy we are putting out. That becomes a step toward healing, or changing, our situation.

When we have a positive attitude, we are able to make the best decisions. Tarot can help us with attitude adjustment and wise decision-making.

Sample Reading: Decision Making

"I need to make a decision by 5 pm today!" Nan said on the phone, breathlessly, at 2 pm.

I looked at the clock and looked at my calendar.

"I simply don't have an opening until this evening, but I can give you ten minutes right now. However, I cannot make a decision for you. You know that, right?"

Nan was grateful for my time, and it seemed that she understood that I could help her evaluate the situation, but that the final decision would be hers.

She briefly told me her situation. She was 25, a college graduate, working full time, and still living at home. Her parents expected her to live at home until she married. Currently, there was no boyfriend. She had a friend who wanted her to move into her apartment and be roommates. She had also found a cute studio apartment that she could easily afford on her own. She had to let the landlord of the apartment know if she would take it or he would give it to someone else.

And so, we began the reading. I shuffled and pulled one card to represent her living with her family, at home, as they expected. The card that came up was the Seven of Swords. I interpreted this in three ways. First, she is not true to herself by continuing to live with her parents. Second, she probably has not yet told her parents that she is considering moving out. Third, she feels guilty, either toward her parents or financially, for moving out.

Next, I pull a card to represent her living in the studio apartment. It is the Nine of Cups. I explain to her that this is the traditional "Wish Card." I also call it the "Fat and Happy Card." To me it seems that living on her own is truly what she wishes to do. Clearly, she can afford it, and it will make her happy. I tell her this, and she seems relieved.

The, I look at the roommate idea. I pull a card to represent the friend. I got the King of Wands reversed.

"Does your friend have a boyfriend?" I ask.

"Yes," she says. "He's a creep."

I had thought we might need to go further, to pull more cards to look at the roommate situation. But she had said it all. If she stayed at home, she would be untrue to herself. If she took the apartment with the roommate she would have to deal with the creepy boyfriend. If she took the studio apartment, she would be content and satisfied.

Nan had been able to draw the conclusion herself, based on what the tarot helped her see.

Tarot Ethics

Every tarot reader, and especially every tarot professional, should have a clear ethics statement. Each reader will define their ethics differently. The important thing is that each reader must understand that they need to put some time and energy into discerning their own sense of tarot ethics.

For instance, I have a colleague who won't read for a person more than once a month. That is part of his commitment to ethics. My ethical commitment is to try to provide readings when they are requested, regardless of the time that has passed.

One point of ethics that seems to be universal is the idea that tarot readers should refer clients to the appropriate professionals when needed. We need to tell a client to see their doctor, rather than trying to make medical diagnoses. We need to tell a client to see their attorney, rather than giving legal advice. When we see depression, we need to refer to a therapist.

Another universal ethic is clear and fair pricing. Whether we work by trade, read for friends for fun, or have a tarot business, we need to be clear about a fair exchange of energy. Even before I was a professional reader, my friends would invite me for dinner, or bring me a small gift. It was never anything I asked for, it is just the way energy works.

As a professional, I see that readers charge in a variety of ways; by the service, by the hour, or by the card. If you choose to read professionally, set a rate structure that is fair and easy to understand.

Perhaps most important is the idea that people do put some faith and trust in tarot professionals, and we should not take unfair advantage of that or betray their trust or confidence in any way.

Ethics Exercise

Pull one card to represent your ethics as a tarot reader. Write about the card you got, and what it means to you.

Now write a statement of ethics directed to your clients, or the friends and family with whom you will share readings. What do you want the people who seek readings with you to know about your ethics and values?

Advanced Exercise: Referrals

Create a list of emergency referral telephone numbers. Include free mammogram programs, child and youth services, a therapist that you trust, a suicide hotline, Planned Parenthood and other area services your clients may need.

Spotting Truth and Untruth in a Reading

There are many cards that can come up to tell you that you are on the right track in a reading and that you know the truth. Likewise, the cards can tell you if someone else is acting in either an honest or a dishonest way. Be careful though, about accusing someone of being dishonest. Sometimes it is better to say that a person does not speak the truth because they do not know their own truth than it is to call a person an out-and-out liar.

Of course, the most prominent card of dishonesty is the Seven of Swords. Some people see the Moon as saying, "Think twice, all is not as it seems." The Seven of Cups can indicate confusion; the Three of Swords can indicate betrayal. Any of the Swords Court reversed can suggest dishonest people, or dishonest communication. The Ace of Swords reversed can suggest that the truth is either not communicated or not known. Justice reversed could indicate unfair treatment.

The Ace of Swords in its upright position can indicate truth and knowledge. Justice upright can indicate fairness. The Six of Swords may suggest that one is one the right track and thinking clearly.

The Page of Cups may suggest that someone is speaking from their heart.

Throughout the course of a reading, it is a good practice to check yourself by silently asking "Am I on the right track? And then pull a card to give you the answer. You can also use a pendulum in the same way.

Stories from the Suit of Swords

What follows are three interesting experiences that I have had with Swords cards.

The first happened when I was teaching an Adult Education class in tarot, very early in my career. I was introducing the students to the Minor Arcana. After going through them card-by-card I said, "Why do you think that the Swords cards have more difficult images than any of the other suits?" A little voice popped up from the back of the room. "The truth hurts," she said.

The second happened not long after that. While doing a spread for a female client, I noticed that the Ace of Swords was in her relationship position. I took it to mean that she and her husband had a very honest relationship. The truth was that she had just discovered her husband was cheating on her. I then realized that the Ace of Swords symbolized her discovery of this unpleasant truth.

A few years after that, I did two readings for someone in the same day. She was my first client that morning. Her problem was that she was trying to decide whether to end her marriage. She was of a mixed mind about it, and the cards weren't helping. Everything pointed to the idea that it was her choice and her choice alone. If she wasn't ready to choose, she would just have to sit with it for a while. Her final card was the Two of Swords, which seemed very fitting. Even though we came to no conclusion, she was so happy with her reading that she came back that evening at about 9 pm. We went through the whole process again, with much the same results, including the very last card which was, once again, the Two of Swords!

Magickal Dedication for your Tarot Journey

Your tarot journey can last a lifetime, and can offer a lifetime of contemplation, wisdom, and insight. If your journey includes reading for others, it can offer you the incomparable feeling of helping others. If your journey takes you to tarot classes or groups, it can give you a strong sense of spiritual community and social opportunities. Wherever your tarot journey takes you, it is certainly a part of your greater spiritual journey.

From time to time, it is good to assess your goals for your journey and make a magickal dedication of yourself as a student of the tarot.

Here's a way to do that. You'll need your tarot cards, your tarot journal, and some incense or herbs to burn, preferably some that is associated with the element of Air. Good choices would be lavender, pine or lemon balm.

To begin, light your incense, and any candles you would like to use. Take a few minutes to breathe, ground and focus.

Sit with your tarot journal and think about your spiritual journey. Write a few lines about where you've been spiritually, where you are now, and where you would like to be going. Now think of a tarot card that describes your current spiritual journey and write about it. Why did you choose this card, and what does it mean to you in this context?

Now, think specifically about your tarot journey, and write about that. Where are you now? Where would you like to be? Think about a card that describes your current relationship with the tarot. Write about it and why you chose it.

Shuffle your deck and think again about your spiritual journey. Pick one card at random. What card did you pick? How does it relate to your spiritual journey? Record the card in your journal and write about the insights it gives you.

Do the same now regarding your tarot journey. Think about your relationship with tarot and pull one card at random. Think about the card you got and write in your journal about it.

Shuffle again and pull a card at random to describe how your work with the tarot aids you on your spiritual journey. Think about the card you got and write about it.

The time has come to write your dedication. By now you should have a pretty good idea of where you are as a tarot student and where you would like to be. Take a moment to write a paragraph that states your goals and intentions as a tarot student. In this paragraph you may ask for assistance from the spirit world, from Higher Power, and from your own higher self. Write about the specific skills you will need to develop and the type of discipline you will need to employ. You may write this in paragraph form, or as a poem, or a prayer.

Once it is written, look through your tarot deck and cognitively pick out some cards that represent the energies that you will need in order to achieve your goals as a tarot student. Choose some cards that represent the goals you have set as well. Lay these cards in front of you and spend some time looking at them, meditating, and breathing in their energy to bring it into yourself.

Now, read your dedication aloud.

The magick begins when you first think about your dedication. It is strengthened when you write it, and manifests when you speak it. Thinking, writing and speaking are all aspects of the Air element.

You may create a new dedication when you have achieved the goals you have set forth in this one.

May the element of Air guide you on your journey.

CHAPTER NINE

The Element of Earth- Grounding, Healing, Home, and Abundance.

This chapter, dedicated to Earth, discusses the use of tarot to aid in the practical matters of the material world. While tarot is a guide on our spiritual journey, it is also a strategic tool to help us stay grounded in earthly reality. It teaches us to see the way spirit moves in our mundane lives as an important part of our spiritual journey.

Most spiritual traditions allow and encourage prayer, meditation or magick to assist in our daily physical struggles for health and abundance.

In Earth-based religions, true spiritual attunement does not begin with the eyes cast toward heaven, it begins with the ability to be grounded and rooted to the Earth.

For all people, our ability to focus on spiritual thought is enhanced when our material needs are met. The lucky few are able to meet their material needs by working in a vocation that is part of their spiritual calling. Others, also blessed, are at least able to see a spiritual purpose within their mundane tasks.

Many people use spiritual practices such as meditation, yoga and dance to help maintain their physical wellness.

Tarot meditation will help us connect with the element of Earth and stay grounded and centered. Tarot divination will help us find and maintain our best career path and our best options for maintaining physical wellness and managing our finances. We can use tarot magick to manifest our desires for appropriate career, material abundance, and good health.

Since Earth rules the material world, we will call on it to help with our grounding, our ability to choose a career path, our ability to work hard, our ability to manifest health and wealth, and our ability to nurture our families and ourselves.

Earth is our connection to our source. In Pagan traditions Mother Earth is acknowledged as our source of strength and our source of being. In Judeo-Christian traditions God created the Earth, fashioned man out of clay, and gave us stewardship of the Earth.

Many spiritual people try to disassociate themselves from their human nature and their connection to the Earth. Truly, it is only through honoring and accepting that earthy connection that we are able to honor our spiritual nature. Earth gives us sustenance and nurturance. It is our home, and our ability to manifest our dreams into solid reality. It is our health, and our ability to connect with our bodies. It is our fertility, and our ability to honor our ancestors and raise our children. Earth rules both birth and death. Earth ties us to that primal circle of life that none can escape. We are made of earth and will return to earth when we die. Earth creates both the strength and the need to accomplish our daily tasks. It is through those daily tasks that we build the structure of our lives.

Invocation of the Earth

The Ace of Pentacles is a magickal tool that invokes Earth. Through this invocation, we bring the energy of Earth to us. We will dedicate tarot as a tool that will help us build our lives. We will build our bodies to be strong and healthy. We will build our homes to be places of refuge, solace, warmth, and comfort. We will build our careers to be satisfying and profitable. We will build our families to be a testament to our heritage and a hope for our future. And we will build our spiritual life based on the solid foundation of the Earth.

Look at your Ace of Pentacles and see it as the core symbol of grounding, stability, physical strength, and material abundance. Stand up and hold the Ace of Pentacles to your solar plexus. Take a deep breath, and as you exhale, send your energy down your body, through your legs, through your feet, and into the Earth. As you continue to breathe, continue to send your energy deep into the Earth. Then, as you inhale, bring energy from the Earth up your legs, through your spine, through your arms, and let it connect with the card that you hold in your hands. Feel the strength of Earth within you and feel yourself as a part of the Earth. Say an invocation, such as the following.

"As I ground myself to the Earth, I bring Earth to my spirit. With this pentacle I bring grounding, healing, stability, and abundance to myself. I honor the tarot as a tool of the Earth that will help me to understand the great circle of life and my place within it. I dedicate my tarot cards, and my study and use of tarot, to the manifestation of health, wealth and abundance in my life, and in the lives of those around me. I honor the Earth as the source of all life and all that I need. I ask the Earth for the courage and strength to work hard, to stay grounded, and to create all I need to feed myself in body, mind, and spirit, and to feed those around me, in body, mind, and spirit.

With this pentacle, and with my strength, I call the powers of Earth. May Earth bring me, and help me to create for myself, all that I need, not only to survive, but to thrive, as I continue on my journey."

Pentacles Earth Exercise

Look at the Pentacles cards two through ten. Each of these cards represents some aspect of wealth and abundance. Look at each card and think about how wealth is portrayed in each one.

From the Pentacles two through ten, choose the cards that represent where you feel you are right now in your journey toward building an abundant life.

Now look at the cards you didn't choose. From them, choose the ones that you would like to set as goals for your further progress. Now look at the remaining cards, those that you still haven't chosen. Do any of these represent aspects of your past, or attitudes that you would like to avoid on your journey toward material success?

Major Arcana Earth Exercise

Place the Major Arcana cards that are traditionally associated with the element of Earth in front of you. They are the Empress, the Hierophant, the Hermit, the Devil, and The World.

Think about these cards in association with the element of Earth.

How does each of these cards symbolize the element of Earth?

What do you learn about Earth when you look at these cards?

What do you learn about each of these cards when you think of it as a symbol of Earth?

Clues for the Beginner- Earth: Taking Care of Your Tarot Cards

Part of Earth energy is to maintain the physical tools in our lives. There are special traditions around the care and maintenance of your tarot deck. First, don't keep your cards in the box that they came in when you bought them. You need to wrap them in material or put them in a pouch or a box. Tradition suggests that they be wrapped in black silk, but this is not strictly necessary.

Second Edition Author Note:

If you have seen any of the phenomenal boxes some new tarot decks are packaged in these days, you know that my admonition to not keep your working cards in their original box is outdated. If your deck came in a tin or a lovely sturdy box it is perfectly okay to keep your cards stored there.

* * *

You may clean your cards physically by gently wiping each card with a slightly damp cloth. You can cleanse them energetically by leaving them on an indoor windowsill in the light of the full moon or burning sage or other incense and bathing them in the smoke.

New readers should sleep with their cards to bond with them. Just put them under your pillow or under your bed. Believe it or not, the cards will influence your dreams when you sleep with them.

Plan your Career with Tarot

Most of my students and tarot friends keep a tarot deck in their desk drawer at work. Just about every one of them carries a deck in their pocketbook or briefcase. Sometimes this is simply to give readings to their co-workers when the boss isn't looking. But often it is because they have figured out that tarot offers a great map through the career jungle.

It is also true that most professional tarot readers will spend a great deal of time counseling their clients on work-related issues. The tarot solutions in this section can help you with your career issues. If you are a professional tarot reader, they can help you help your clients keep on the right career track.

Career is a strong part of some people's spiritual path. Finding and maintaining that career is an essential part of their identity and spiritual nature. Others turn to spirituality to find the strength to tolerate a difficult, but necessary, job. For some, the spiritual calling will not be a paying job, but something on a creative, homemaking or volunteer basis.

Whether the goal is spiritual fulfillment, finding one's true talent or simply paying the bills, tarot is a creative and practical career tool.

Finding Your Calling

What do you want to be when you grow up? This question comes up repeatedly in my professional readings and usually for people over the age of forty.

I also do many readings for graduating high school seniors at their school-sponsored safe graduation parties. Of course, the topic of career choice comes up in their readings quite frequently.

The amazing thing is that I've seen a great deal of similarity between the perspective of the eighteen-year-old just starting out and the forty-five-year-old starting over. It seems the idea that a person will have just one career in their lifetime may be as passé as sock hops and gramophones.

Yet, one eternal thing is that most everyone wants a career that sings to their heart. Another eternal truth is that it is difficult at any age to choose such a path, and more difficult still to make it happen. Tarot can be a great tool for discovering passions, finding paths, and solving the practical problems along the way.

Sometimes we are consciously aware that we need to discover our passion or hear our calling. Other times, we are so distracted by our day-to-day responsibilities that we can't even imagine the possibility of a truly meaningful career. Sometimes cards in a general reading will tell you that career needs to be a focus. Other times you will have direct questions about career planning.

The card that clearly speaks to me of "hearing a calling" is the Major Arcana card 20, Judgment. The standard Waite image of Judgment includes an angel blowing a horn. This to me is the spiritual calling that leads to the perfect career. There are other Major Arcana cards that speak to me of the search for the right career, such as the Fool and the Moon, which both indicate the need to find one's path. Pentacles cards can indicate career concerns. The Seven of Pentacles may indicate boredom with one's job. The Five of Pentacles may suggest that one is not being paid what one is worth or is not being allowed to perform the tasks to which they are best suited.

Many cards speak of education, which is often a primary component of career achievement. The Magician, the Eight of Pentacles, the Three of Pentacles, the Knight of Swords and all the Pages can all speak of being a student or an apprentice. The Hierophant and the Hermit can speak specifically of higher education, or of a career as an educator.

But what about someone who wants a career about which they are passionate, but tells you they have no idea of what they might enjoy or in what they might do well? This happens very often, and usually, after I look at the cards and pinpoint an area of interest or a specific talent, the client will say "I've thought of that," or "that's my dream job," or "that's what I studied in college." Then the challenge is to figure out why they hadn't identified this as their passionate career, or what obstacles they feel are insurmountable. Often, it is simply fear. Fear that they won't be successful, or that they aren't talented enough in that area. The reader needs to be able to realistically access the situation. Perhaps the career goal really isn't appropriate, and a new one needs to be discovered. Or perhaps it is the perfect goal, and fear needs to be replaced with confidence and vision.

There are many ways to identify interests or talents with the cards. The Hierophant, either upright or reversed, may refer to an educator, a manager, or a business owner. It may also represent clergy or medicine. Justice may indicate someone involved with the law or legalities. The Eight of Pentacles may be a tradesperson. The Three of Pentacles may be a craftsperson. The Six of Pentacles may involve medicine, social work or psychology. The Emperor may come up for someone who is good with math and numbers, such as a banker or accountant. The High Priestess and the Hermit may come up for folks who work best on their own, rather than as part of a group.

Traditionally, the Nine of Cups is the "Happy Merchant," so he may show up for someone who is good in retail or who should own a shop. The Nine of Pentacles and the Seven of Pentacles often feature gardens in their images, so they may indicate someone who is good with plants. Strength may indicate a person who is good with animals. The Empress may suggest a person is good with children.

The Chariot, and the Knights, may indicate a professional driver, or one whose job should include travel. The Ten of Pentacles may indicate real estate, or a builder or developer. The Three of Cups may indicate a dancer or a musician. The Sun may indicate a performer. The Six of Wands may indicate an athlete.

Card combinations matter a great deal here. For instance, the Six of Wands, as the card of victory, and the Chariot, as the warrior, and the Hierophant, as the card of order and tradition, may appear together to describe the qualities of a soldier. However, if you see the Hierophant with the High Priestess, who is wise, knowledgeable and precise, and the Six of Pentacles, which denotes charity, or helping people, you may be looking at a medical professional.

Career Cards Exercise

Look at the cards I have given as examples above and decide if you see the careers and talents I describe in them. If so, why? If not, what careers seem like a better fit for each card? Now, go through your deck, card by card, and think of a career or talent that matches each card.

Exercise for the Advanced Student- Real Life Career

Think of people you know who have very definite and passionate careers. One at a time, pull a card at random to describe each person's career, and see what you get. Now pull a card for each person to see how they feel about their career at present. Do those cards match your guesses or do they give you insight you hadn't expected?

Tarot Magick to Find Your Calling

In addition to using tarot divination to find your calling, you can also use tarot magick.

Start with the Judgment card, and any candles or incense you prefer to create sacred space. Arrange your candles and incense around the Judgment card, leaving plenty of room for the other cards you will use. As you light the candles and incense, breathe deeply. Let go of your worries and concerns. Focus on the Judgment card and realize that before you can hear the call of the angel, you will need to be receptive and open. As you breathe, concentrate on being open to guidance from a Higher Power.

Next, you will need to be open to knowing your own talents, skills and abilities. As you breathe out, let go of your insecurities. Let go of any ideas you have that you simply can't do something or can't be successful.

Now, look through your tarot deck, which should be complete except for Judgment, which is already in front of you. Breathe, and focus on what you already know about yourself, and about what your perfect job might be. Even if you can't figure out what the actual job is, think about tasks you have done in your life and enjoyed. Think

Tarot Tour Guide

about skills you have, and the times that you have felt proudest using your skills. Think of the times you have won admiration from others.

As you think about these things, cognitively choose one card from each of the four suits to illustrate aspects of your talents and skills, and the sorts of tasks or environments you enjoy.

Place those four cards around the Judgment card and focus on them for a moment. Think about what it will be like when your day-to-day work reflects what you see in these images.

Now look through the deck again, looking at the Major Arcana cards. Is there a card amongst them that reflects the energy you would like to feel as part of your career? If so, place it on the table with the other cards.

Choose a Court card that represents who you are at present, and place it on the table, but away from the other cards you have chosen. Now, think about the Court card that would best represent you if you were using all your skills and abilities and happy in your ideal career. Take that Court card and place it on the table with the other cards you have chosen. Take the original Court card that you chose to represent you and move it to the group of cards. As you do that, say something like this.

"This card represents me. These cards represent my ideal career, which is my spiritual calling and my mission in this lifetime. As I place this card with these others, I am affirming that I am ready and worthy to hear, understand and follow my calling. I know that my calling will be made clear to me quickly, and that I will have the means and the opportunity to follow it easily and with joy. For this I am grateful."

Sit with the cards for as long as you like, visualizing yourself in a job that suits you perfectly.

Mapping the Path

Once you define the skills, talents and ambitions that you have you can use tarot to come up with a plan to get on the right path.

Start by simply shuffling the deck, and asking the question, "What is the first step toward achieving this career goal?"

Pull one card and interpret it to answer the question.

Next, here is a list of the next questions you will need to ask. Each can be handled by pulling a card or pulling a few cards.

What is the potential for success with the goal?
What fears might hold me back?
What will I have to give up in order to achieve this goal?
How will the people around me help me to achieve this goal?
Where is there support for me of which I might not be aware?
What specific skills should I be developing?
What will be the most difficult part of this process?
What will be the greatest rewards of following this path?

A Sample Reading using the Mapping the Path Questions

Maria, a regular client, asked for a phone reading because she was considering taking a huge and daunting career step. She wanted to quit her job in the social services field and focus on being an artist, an energy healer, and a yoga instructor. We both felt that these three fields could meld together well. In many ways it was about Maria finding a way to get paid for simply being Maria! We discussed venues, different sorts of classes that she could teach, including art classes and healing classes. We discussed ways to incorporate art into healing work, and to market services that encompassed all three areas. Once we had a clear understanding of Maria's goals as she saw them, we began the reading.

Question 1. What is the first step toward achieving this career goal?"

Answer: Strength

I thought it was very auspicious to have a Major Arcana card here, and such a good one. I told her that she would need to believe that she had the strength and skill to do this. She would need to do it with love in her heart; love for her work and love for her clients. She would need to find balance between the need to market aggressively, like the lion, and the need to be sweet and gentle to everyone she encountered, like the woman.

Question 2. What is the potential for success with the goal?

Answer: Ten of Cups

Again, a very positive card, the Ten of Cups indicates that she could have wonderful success. She might not become rich, but she could certainly make enough money to make it worthwhile. This could make her very happy, and could give her the opportunity to make others happy as well.

Question 3. What fears might hold me back?

Answer: Page of Swords

This could be interpreted in a few ways. Maria has one young child, and so I chose to see it as Maria's very legitimate fear that she wouldn't have enough time or money to support her child while she was building her business. I also felt it could be a fear of not communicating appropriately, of not marketing well enough, or of not having enough knowledge either of business or of her subject matter.

Question 4. What will I have to give up in order to achieve this goal?

Answer: Judgment

Hmm... This is interesting, since I do see Judgment as the card of "hearing your calling," and also of rebirth. Both are positive things, not anything that would be given up in this situation. I told Maria what had come up, since she was on the phone and couldn't see the card. I explained to her that it was a very positive card but didn't seem to answer the question. She asked me if the Judgment card could ever refer to being judgmental of others. While that is not a meaning I tend to see in it, I know other readers who do. She started laughing and said that made sense to her. She had been feeling very judgmental of others recently and knew that was not an appropriate energy for one who wanted to be a spiritual healer and teacher. I agreed that would certainly be something she needed to give up!

Question 5: Where is there support for me of which I might not be aware?

Answer: Three of Cups

I often see this card as a reference to female friends. It can also be a card of parties and social gatherings. I told her that her girlfriends could be counted on to both help with babysitting and also with getting the word out about her services, classes and events. I also suggested that she organize "parties" where she could offer services or workshops.

Question 6: What specific skills should I be developing?

Answer: Ten of Wands

This is the first difficult card that has come up during this reading. The Ten of Wands speaks of the ability to exert a herculean effort and sustain it for as long as necessary. Maria needs to develop discipline, the ability to handle a great number of tasks on her own, and the ability to work tirelessly for as long as it takes, even when those around her are at rest or at play.

Question Seven: What will be the most difficult part of this process?

Answer: Nine of Pentacles, Reversed

This is the first reversed card in this reading. In its reversal it speaks of insecurity. Maria's biggest problem will be battling the feeling of financial insecurity, and the feeling that she may not be skilled enough to do this, even though in her heart she knows she is. Some of this insecurity may come from the words and actions of others. Family members, friends, and colleagues may question her decisions, and cause her to feel constantly defensive and insecure in her decision to follow her path. Her ability to counter this will be a deciding factor in her ability to be successful.

Question Nine: What will be the greatest rewards of following this path?

Answer: Seven of Pentacles Reversed.

A reversed card answers the last question. Interesting that the first few cards of this reading were so strong, profound and positive, and the last few, at first glance, seem less so. As we look at this final card, however, it seems to make a lot of sense. Maria's greatest reward will be that she will no longer have to work a "regular job." She will not have to do work that seems endless, meaningless or dull. She would rather work hard and earn less doing something creative on her own terms than sit in a secure position doing something that doesn't really match her integrity, creativity, and calling.

I suggest that she use this as a self-motivator when times get tough.

From this reading, we learn that Maria has good ideas, skills, and the support of some of her friends. Her biggest challenges will be to discipline herself and to develop the ability to believe in herself and her business even in the face of others' doubts. She must always exhibit the attitude appropriate for a spiritual teacher and mentor, even when she doesn't feel like it. Her biggest motivator will be her distaste for the limitations presented by a traditional job.

In terms of practical advice, this reading suggests that she create and seek out social gatherings as places to find clientele and present programs. She needs to pay special attention to "getting the word out," and she needs to enlist her friends to help her create a buzz about her business.

You can see from Maria's reading that the Mapping the Path method offers insight into many aspects of career development. In this case, hidden issues that are deeply personal and psychological play as big a role as the practical issues of time management and marketing.

This is one of the reasons that tarot is such an effect tool for career exploration. Tarot can help us look at the most important aspects of any situation. It will always reveal the bare bones truth about our best skills and our deepest fears and flaws.

A Sample Career Reading

Darla, who is in her early 50s, had made an appointment for an hour-long reading. She is a regular client, so I knew something about her job and family background. She asked one question, spontaneously, before we began the reading. It involved telling me about some dreams and other experiences she had been having. These experiences seemed to both of us to be valid out-of-body and spirit communication experiences. She was intently focused on dealing with these experiences, which included communication with relatives in spirit who had given her knowledge of a death in the family just days before it occurred. As I shuffled and laid out the opening spread (my usual eleven-card Celtic Cross) the cards that came up were not the ones I had expected to see. I had expected some Major Arcana, to describe the spiritual nature of her recent experiences and questions about them. I expected some Cups cards, to describe her intuition and her emotions around that, and around having had both contact from the Other Side and a recent death in the family. I expected some Wands to describe the energy running through her, and maybe some aces and Queens to describe these new beginnings, new energies and new aspects of her identity.

What I got were a whole lot of Pentacles. Out of the eleven cards, eight were Pentacles! There was only one Major Arcana, which was the Sun, in the position of love and romance. She has a great marriage, so that was not a surprise. Her daughter, who had recently announced her engagement, showed up as the Knight of Cups in the Crown position. The Ten of Cups showed up in her Atmosphere position, not surprising given her wonderful family.

Since Darla is also a tarot student, I commented on the vast number of Pentacles, which she had also noticed. We talked about the very positive cards that indicated her family, and I was able to tie that in to her experience with her family members in spirit. Clearly, it seemed that both her family on Earth and her family in spirit created a loving presence around her.

But what about all those Pentacles cards? There were so many of them it was hard to focus on just one. I suggested that we needed to speak about her career, and she agreed. The significator was the Two of Pentacles, and that seemed, well, significant, so I started with that. "Are you working a second job, or considering another career?" I asked. "Not really," she said. Darla had worked for a large corporation in a fairly good position for as long as I had known her, and I had always thought she was relatively happy there. I said so. "But," I said, "we can't ignore what we see here. Something is definitely going on career-wise."

"Well, "she said, "I have been thinking about taking on a volunteer job working with the terminally ill. Also, I keep wondering if I should stay where I am until I retire, or if I should take early retirement and do something else. I am at that age, you know, where I wonder- is this all there is for me?"

Aha! Now everything started to make sense, and I quickly put it together for her. Her dreams and recent psychic experiences suggest a time of spiritual growth and attunement that often happens at the "cronetime," when a woman reaches the age of 50 or so. In the mundane world, that timing corresponds with what is really the last chance to make a career change before it is simply too late. Combining that with the obvious doldrums that I see in her current job (Two of Pentacles, Seven of Pentacles, Five of Pentacles) and her recent excitement to volunteer with the terminally ill, I think it's time to make a suggestion.

"Have you ever thought of going back to school, to be trained for a career you would find more fulfilling, and more in line with your spiritual calling?"

"I have thought about it. I thought about maybe being a dental assistant."

"That is certainly a great career. But let's look at what has been happening. Your departed loved ones appear to you and tell you about an impending family bereavement. Then you receive an opportunity to work with the terminally ill for no money and that sounds good to you. Could it be that the universe is trying to tell you something? Could it be that your calling, that your gift, will involve working with those who are dying, or those who are grieving?"

She seems to light up when I said this, but then said, "isn't that a little creepy, to want to work with people like that?"

"No one says it's creepy when someone wants to be a midwife and help to usher folks into the world," I said. "Why should it be creepy to help a family with another of life's cycles?"

Then, I pulled three cards. They were the Hermit, the High Priestess and the Nine of Pentacles. We spoke for a long time about those three cards. She had some interesting insights about them and related them to another piece of her family history, the death of a sibling. While I certainly hadn't seen that correlation, she did, and that was what was important. All her experiences; leadership in the corporate world, family bereavement, deeply personal psychic and spiritual experiences, and even the study of tarot and attendance at the Presbyterian Church, seemed to lead her to a single place, but a place she had not been able to see before this reading. The final piece came together when we realized that she had enough time before she could take her early retirement to attend and complete school.

For me, the High Priestess and the Hermit both spoke of education, and specifically that which would involve the deep spiritual mysteries, of which death is certainly one. Both cards also spoke of her ability to share knowledge with others, especially from a spiritual perspective. The Nine of Pentacles told me that she was coming from a secure position, that she would have the time, money and support to do this if she chose. Since the Hermit is also a nine, I thought about the number nine as being about satisfaction and security. I also thought that she could take nine months and no longer to make her decision and take action to begin her education and start the journey toward her calling.

Divination and Magick for Getting a Job

Sometimes we just need a job that will give us a paycheck. Sometimes what matters are the hours, salary or benefits. Perhaps our primary current mission is to go to school, or take care of kids, or write a book. What we need then is an acceptable job.

Perhaps we have finished our education and are ready to begin our grown-up career. No matter what, the next step is getting that first job.

Tarot magick and tarot divination can be invaluable in the search for a job.

Often, as we search for a job, we are plagued with many questions. When will I get a job? Where should I look? What sort of job should I look for? How should I present myself in the interview?

Insights and answers are just a tarot card away. You can do a spread, or simply dialogue with the cards to create an action plan. A heads-up from the cards about the best place to look, or the best way to present yourself, can be invaluable.

There are many ways to use tarot magick to get a job. Simply carry the Ace of Pentacles in your wallet or pocket when you go to an interview. Cognitively find and pull cards related to the sort of job you want and lay them on your tarot altar. Visualize yourself working, driving to work, or depositing your paycheck.

Think about the things that have kept you from working, from loving your job or from getting hired. Cognitively find tarot cards that represent those difficult or negative factors in your life. Put those cards face down on your altar, and as you do, loudly exclaim that you are letting go of your insecurity, or laziness, or whatever else the impediment might be.

Then place cards that you identify as positive work cards face up on your altar.

Cards that represent positive work situations could include the Ace of Pentacles, the Three of Pentacles, the Eight of Pentacles, the Emperor, the Hierophant, the Knight of Pentacles and the King of Pentacles. Be encouraged when you see them come up in readings and use these cards in your get-a-job tarot magick.

Career Shifting Spread

Use this quick spread when considering a new job or a new direction.

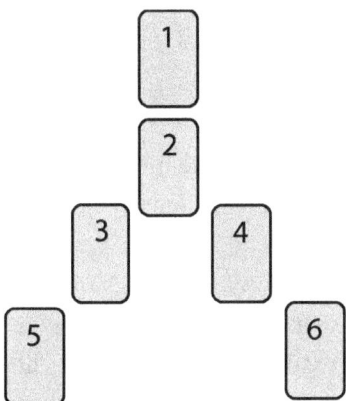

Figure 7 - Career Shifting Spread

Card 1: Your ultimate goal.

Card 2: Where you are right now.

Card 3: What you like about where you are right now.

Card 4: What you don't like about where you are right now.

Card 5: The addition, change or shift that you would prefer.

Card 6: The addition, change or shift that is possible.

Tarot and the Physical Body

Many people consult the tarot to answer questions about health and wellness. It is true that health issues can show up in tarot readings. However, it is very important to refer clients to a medical doctor for all medical advice. That said, it is helpful to know how issues of the body show up in a reading.

Tarot Tour Guide

Second Edition Author Note:

I think what I was awkwardly saying here is that a referral to a proper medical authority is necessary but doesn't preclude the possibility of addressing health concerns with tarot additionally. Tarot can be wonderful for devising coping strategies and finding inspiration during difficult times.

Further, tarot isn't a diagnostic tool. However, sometimes health issues will appear in the cards unbidden.

※ ※ ※

The presence of health issues may be shown by the Hierophant, who can be read as a doctor or the medical establishment. The Three of Swords can represent heart or lung issues. The Ten of Swords can represent back problems. The Eight of Swords can represent clinical anxiety, but also problems with the legs or feet. The Moon and the Seven of Cups can represent mental illness, as can the Devil. The Two of Pentacles can indicate issues of breast health, and fatigue can be represented by the Ace of Wands reversed and the Four of Swords. Weight issues are indicated by the Six of Pentacles and Justice. A refusal to seek medical help might show up as the Five of Pentacles.

When reading for a person whom you suspect of having a health issue, encourage them to see a doctor. When reading for a person who has a known and chronic health issue, ask questions of the cards such as "What is the spiritual purpose of this condition?" And "What can this person do to help themselves heal?"

Occasionally, I have heard from clients who tell me that my insistence that they see a doctor caught a problem before it became serious. While tarot readers simply cannot take responsibility for the physical well-being of others, it is gratifying when our path allows us to help someone along the way.

Second Edition Author Note:

There are other times when a dire illness or physical threat won't make itself known in the cards at all. The fact that sometimes the cards give life-saving information and other times remain frustratingly silent can be heartbreaking. We readers see what we see and must trust that the universe shares what will serve a greater purpose and hides from us what won't.

* * *

Tarot and Attitudes about Money

I've come to believe that peoples' attitudes about money influence their financial status, just as the circumstances of their birth, education and skills do. People who see themselves as successful are successful, and people who are comfortable with money have money. Tarot can help us check our attitudes about money, so that we can be sure we are doing everything possible to create our abundance.

Some people are nervous about money even when they have plenty. Other people spend when they shouldn't. Others feel that money is the root of all evil and shouldn't be a goal. Still others believe that money is the most important goal of all.

Knowing how attitudes about money show up in tarot will help you give solid readings to others and better understand your own financial strengths and weaknesses.

Of course, the first card that we think about is the miser card, the Four of Pentacles. But that card can also indicate a need to save money, or fear and insecurity about money, as well as true miserliness.

The Five of Pentacles suggests poverty or a feeling of impoverishment. Some people feel impoverished even when they are not!

The Six of Pentacles is charity and generosity. The querent may be either the giver or the receiver of the charity.

The Nine of Pentacles suggests an attitude of financial security. This may come from the presence of family money.

The Fool could represent inappropriate spending.

Any of the Pentacles Court cards could represent people who are financially comfortable and happy with their work. When the Pentacles Court is reversed, the opposite may be true on both counts.

When reading for others, and in your own life, be on the lookout for differences in attitudes about money between romantic partners and between parents and their adult children. So often differences in Earth energy (money and resources) get in the way of Water energy (love and relationships)!

Stories from the Suit of Pentacles

While I was running a psychic fair, I was walking through the group of people waiting for readings and mingling. As I was talking with folks, I was absent-mindedly shuffling my tarot cards. One card flew out of the deck and landed at the foot of a woman. Embarrassed that I dropped a card, I picked it up and interpreted it for her. It was the Ace of Pentacles, and so I told her that she would soon have a new job. She said that was very unlikely.

She attended the next fair I presented to tell me about her new job.

While living in an antique home, I came home from the morning's readings to find my husband trying to fix the ancient radiator in the bedroom. He told me it was going to be difficult to fix, and if it couldn't be fixed we wouldn't have heat until he was able to get a special part. I wasn't happy to hear this. For me, heat is essential during a Pocono Mountain winter!

Later that day I was musing on some key words from Aleister Crowley's Thoth Tarot. I was struck, for some reason, by the key word for the Three of Pentacles, which is Works, not Work but Works.

Back at the office, I was wondering about our radiator, and whether I would be going home to a warm house or not. I shuffled and pulled a card. I got the Three of Pentacles. "It Works!" I said.

And it did.

Tarot Magick for Abundance and Wellness

Place on your altar the Ten of Pentacles, the Nine of Pentacles, the Ace of Wands and the Three of Wands. Add to that any other cards that represent wealth and health to you. Strengthen your magick by burning green or brown candles, and incense that is sacred to Earth, such as patchouli, cedar, amber or pine.

Visualize yourself and your home, full of warmth and prosperity. Breathe in and feel yourself grounded to the Earth. See yourself as well, healthy and financially secure. Have faith in your physical security and your own ability to protect, nurture and care for yourself.

Look at each of the cards on the altar. Pick each one up, one at a time, and say what it is you want the card to bring you. For instance, you might say:

Let the Ace of Wands bring me vitality and vigor!

Let the Three of Wands bring success to all my ventures!

Let the Nine of Pentacles bring me security!

Let the Ten of Pentacles bring me a safe and happy home!

Return to your visualization. Leave the cards on the altar overnight.

The magick begins as soon as you ground yourself to the Earth and feel your visualizations as real and tangible.

May Earth bless you on your journey.

CHAPTER TEN

The Element of Water- Love, Sensitivity, Emotion and the Healing Heart.

This chapter, dedicated to Water, discusses the use of tarot to aid in matters of love, and in communicating with the subconscious mind to find emotional balance and healing.

Tarot has long held the reputation of being the panacea of the lovelorn, and with some good reason. Tarot offers an opportunity for us to examine our feelings and to find ways to express them. The predictive aspect of tarot is helpful as we look to the future hoping for healing, happiness, and love.

But love is so much more than romance! The ancient Greeks had many words for love. These included *agape*, meaning spiritual fellowship, *philia*, meaning the loyalty of friendship, and *storge*, which is familial affection. Water rules over all aspects of love and bestows all these gifts to us.

Love is not the only human emotion, but it is the highest expression of human spirituality. In the New Testament, 1 John 4:7-8 says "God is love." We learn that to know God, we must know love.

Oceans cover most of our planet. Their depth and width are beyond most human understanding. As it is with water, so it is with love, and with our capacity for human emotion.

Sometimes our human emotions are our human frailty. Jealously, selfishness, apathy, and sadness clutter our hearts and limit our happiness and success. Water, when we summon it, offers cleansing, refreshment, and the chance to heal and start again.

Psychotherapy, introspection, counseling and shamanic healing are often employed to help find emotional healing and balance. The tarot can be an important adjunct to these modalities in the search for inner peace.

Tarot magick can be used to facilitate emotional healing, strengthen relationships and bring love. In fact, it is the emotion that we put into our magick that strengthens it and gives it energy.

Water represents the deepest part of ourselves; the subconscious, and our higher consciousness. Tarot facilitates communication between the conscious mind, the subconscious mind, and the higher self.

We call on Water to help us understand and manage our emotions and our emotional growth. We use the tarot as a mirror to help us see ourselves, our situations, our relationships, and our emotions more clearly.

Invocation of Water

The Ace of Cups is a magickal tool that invokes Water. Through this invocation we bring the energy of Water to us, and we dedicate the tarot as a tool that will help us to understand the deep subconscious, the higher consciousness, and the spiritual nature of love. We will find healing for our emotional hurts and understanding and love for ourselves. We will find the ability to connect with others in love, in work, and in commonality of purpose. As we open ourselves to Water, we avail ourselves of its healing and cleansing nature.

Look at your Ace of Cups. See it as the core symbol of the open heart, unconditional love, spiritual cleansing, and emotional healing. Stand up and hold the Ace of Cups to your heart. Take a deep breath and visualize yourself at the ocean. Think about the rhythm of the tide, and the waves, and as you stand quietly, feel the rhythms of your own body, all ruled by Water. Say an invocation, such as the following.

"As I open myself to Water, I bring Water to my spirit. With this cup I bring love, cleansing, healing, and compassion to my heart. I honor tarot as a tool of Water that will help me to understand the deeper mysteries of love and the subconscious, and my own ability to love without limitation. I dedicate my tarot cards as a tool that will help me to know love and express love to the world around me.

With this cup and with my heart, I call the powers of Water. May Water bring me healing, love, and the deepest level of spiritual understanding as I continue on my journey."

Cups Water Exercise

Look at the Cup cards two through ten. Each of these cards represents some aspect of emotion. Look at each card and think about what emotion is portrayed in each one.

From the Cups two through ten, choose the cards that represent where you feel you are right now in your journey toward emotional well-being.

Now look at the cards you didn't choose. From them, choose the ones that you would like to set as goals for your further progress. Now look at the remaining cards. Do any of these represent aspects of your past, or attitudes that you would like to avoid on your journey toward emotional well-being?

Major Arcana Water Exercise

Place the Major Arcana cards that are traditionally associated with the element of Water in front of you. They are the High Priestess, the Chariot, the Hanged Man, Death, and The Moon.

Think about these cards in association with what you know about the element of Water.

How does each of these cards symbolize the element of Water?
What do you learn about Water when you look at these cards?
What do you learn about each of these cards when you think of it as a symbol of Water?

Clues for the Beginner- A Two-Card Relationship Spread

It is easy to do a relationship reading using only two cards. Simply shuffle, and say one person's name, and pull a card. Shuffle again, then say the name of the other person and pull a card. Think about how each card reflects each person. Then think about how the two cards interact with each other. How are they similar, and different? What conclusions can you draw about the relationship of the people based on the relationship of the cards? What do you think about the way the cards represent the individuals within the relationship?

Tarot, Self Esteem and Relationships

In a tarot reading, the reader must discern the querent's relationship with his or her self, in other words, the querent's level of self-esteem. How we react to other people, how we succeed at our work and in our relationships can all be driven by our self-esteem. Often, the most critical relationship to be discussed in a reading, and the relationship that needs the most work, is the querent's relationship with self.

Many tarot cards can speak of one's self-image or one's feelings about oneself. When we are contemplating the tarot for our own enlightenment, these cards will often point the way to better self-esteem and a better sense of personal security.

Major Arcana six, the Lovers, is often thought to be about love relationships and discernment. Another meaning for the Lovers is self-esteem. A lesson of the Lovers is that it is impossible to love another until we love ourselves.

In the Minor Arcana, the Two of Cups is very similar to the Lovers and can echo its meaning in this context as well. I often see the Two of Cups as "being a good partner to yourself."

Either of these cards reversed might indicate poor self-esteem. In their upright position they may indicate positive self-esteem and self-image.

Likewise, the Nine of Pentacles, which can be a card of financial security, can also be a card of emotional security. When reversed, we see insecurity.

The Six of Wands may describe someone who is competitive, one who likes the recognition of winning. When reversed, it may be someone who feels like a loser.

The Seven of Swords could suggest that a person does not feel worthy or acceptable.

It's no surprise that people with bad self-esteem often end up having bad love relationships. Of course, there are many cards that describe love and love relationships, and just as many that can speak of trouble in relationships.

When Court cards come up in a spread to represent specific people who share a relationship it can be easy to ascertain the energy of that relationship. First, are the Court cards facing each other, facing the same direction, or facing away from each other?

Are either reversed? If the cards are facing away from each other, or if one is reversed, there is probably some difficultly in the relationship, especially where communication is concerned. Next, what is the rank of the cards? Do the cards reflect their traditional genders? This can tell you if there is a dominant personality in the relationship, and the balance of power within the relationship.

Finally, look at the suits of the Court cards. Are they elements that go together well, like Fire and Air? Or are they elements that oppose each other, like Fire and Water?

As you think about the positioning, elements and ranks of the Court cards involved you will get a more detailed picture of the relationship in question.

There are many cards that speak about relationships. The Hierophant, as a priest, can indicate marriage. The Lovers, of course, can indicate a love relationship. The Star can indicate a sexually satisfying relationship, while the Hermit can indicate loneliness.

In the Minor Arcana, the Two of Cups, the Ten of Cups, and the Ten of Pentacles can also speak of romantic relationships. The Ten of Pentacles can also speak of familial relationships. The Four of Wands is the traditional marriage card. The Six of Cups can indicate a relationship with a long history, or a new relationship with a strong sense of comfort and familiarity. Many people see the Six of Cups signifying a soulmate or past life connection in a love relationship.

Some tarot cards can also give a sense of how romantic partners feel about each other. For example, if a gentleman receives the High Priestess to describe his wife, we know that he feels he is with a woman who is perfect for him. The Emperor in a woman's reading may suggest that she finds her partner to be very stable and dependable.

Wands cards can often speak of arguments. The Ace of Wands itself can speak of anger. The Seven of Wands may describe a defensive attitude within a relationship that makes communication difficult. The Five of Wands can indicate conflict in a relationship, while the Nine of Wands can indicate a long-standing disagreement.

Other suits may also give insight into relationship dynamics. The Four of Pentacles may discuss selfish behavior or poor boundaries, while the Three of Swords is the traditional card of the lover's triangle. The Four of Swords might suggest the lack of a relationship, or a relationship with very little communication or intimacy.

Some cards can speak of friendship, such as the Three of Cups, which depicts a social gathering. The Seven of Wands reversed can also suggest a strong and helpful friend, as does the Hermit reversed and the Nine of Wands reversed.

Tarot can help us find the words to describe our most confusing relationships. It can also help us to build our self-esteem, and to celebrate the beautiful connections in our lives.

Exercise for the Advanced Student: Court Card Relationships

Separate out your Court cards and shuffle them. Arrange them in random pairs. Make up stories about the different relationships that you see between the characters in each pair.

Tarot Fellowship and Group Dynamics

Tarot fosters fellowship and draws good people together. Tarot is a wonderful tool for group-building, and for understanding the dynamics of any group.

To discover the dynamics of a group, pull one card for each of the participants. If you are reading for a group who is present, have each member pull their own card. Look at the cards and see what each card says about the role each person places in the group. See how the cards interact together, and you'll get a feeling for the dynamics of the group overall.

Building fellowship amongst tarot enthusiasts is as easy as using a social networking website or posting a notice at your local book store or cafe. When you get a tarot group together, it is fun to do exercises that are entertaining and insightful, like the ones that follow.

Second Edition Author Note:

Clearly social media has developed a bit since I wrote this. As I prepare this second edition, I can see how much active and vibrant Facebook Tarot groups like Tarot Nerds and Tarot Professionals have added to my own understanding of tarot and sense of community. Meetup and Facebook events continue to be a worthwhile way to bring tarot groups together for in-person fellowship.

Over the next few years digital communication will advance again. Whatever technology brings us next, I am sure it will offer us new ways for us to read for each other, study tarot together and enjoy the company of our tarot friends around the world.

* * *

Group Exercises

Tarot works equally well as a solitary pursuit, one-on-one, or in a group. The following exercises are designed specifically for groups and classes. Each exercise works to promote a specific tarot skill. All the exercises are designed to promote fun, fellowship and community building around the tarot.

Storytelling

Each group member draws four cards from their deck at random and places them in a row. Looking at the pictures on the cards, rather than their traditional interpretations, each member quickly and extemporaneously composes a story based on the four cards and shares it with the group.

Circle Definitions

The group sits in a circle, each member with their own tarot deck. Each deck must be in the same order. Going around the circle, the first player gives a short definition, phrase or key words for the top card. The next person to the left defines the next card, and so on, in order, for all seventy-eight cards.

This game should move quickly. If a player can't define the card, the play passes to the next person. This game is particularly helpful for students who are working on card memorization.

Tarot Charades

This game is both very profound and very silly. It requires the players to, one at a time, silently act out a Major Arcana card. As in regular charades, the rest of the group must guess the card that is being embodied.

Round Robin Readings

This exercise teaches us to ask proper questions of the tarot. It also promotes the skill of "mini-readings," or pulling just a few cards to answer a question.

Sitting in a circle, each player has his or her own deck. The first player will ask a question of the person on their left. The person on their left will pull a card, or a few cards from their deck, show those cards to the rest of the group, and use those cards to answer the question. The play continues as that person then asks a question of the person to his/her left, and so on. The group can add their insight to each reading. Questions should be specific, personal, and not terribly embarrassing.

Introductions

This exercise is good for new groups of proficient readers. Use it as an "ice-breaker" or first exercise.

Divide the group into partners, preferably who do not know each other. Each person gets five minutes to read for his or her partner. From that reading, they must glean as much information about their partner as possible. Once everyone has read for each other, each person will introduce their partner to the group, sharing the information that they derived from the reading.

On Your Mind

The group sits in a circle. Each person has his or her own tarot deck. Players take turns being "It." "It" must, at random, draw one card from their deck. Without looking at the card, "It" must hold the card to his or her forehead, so that the group can see the card, but "It" cannot. Members of the group interpret the card without saying its name. The card will speak to whatever is most on "Its" mind at the current time. "It" must accept the reading from the group and must guess which card he or she is holding.

Predicting and Finding Romance with Tarot

We all know the stereotype. The lonely woman, in desperation, visits the fortune teller. With a dramatic gesture, the fortune teller tells her that she will meet a tall, dark handsome stranger.

Whether or not this is an accurate portrayal of a modern tarot reading, it does make an obvious point.

Everyone is looking for love. Well, not everyone. But there sure are a lot of single people hoping to meet the right person. No doubt, if you are a tarot reader, some of them will find their way to your table.

The sad truth of the matter that is evidenced to us every day is that there is not someone for everyone. It is also true, though, that the most unlikely people find love in the most unusual places. When you have a single friend or client asking for predictions about love for the future, you need to strike the right balance of hope, practicality, and legitimate divination.

I generally begin a consultation about finding love with a series of questions for the cards in order to ascertain the likelihood that my querent will indeed be meeting a person of interest soon.

The first question is, "Is there anyone that is now known to my querent who could be a possibility?" I ask the question aloud, shuffle, and pull as many cards as feels right. In the cards I look for clues about a person who might be a friend, a co-worker or acquaintance that may have an interest or be a good choice. I look for Court cards to represent possible suitors. Often, I see folks who are interested, but when I mention them to the querent, the querent identifies them as people who have expressed interest that the querent does not find attractive or appropriate. In this case I will pull a few more cards to see if I agree that the person is not right for the querent. If I do agree, I simply move on to the next question. If I don't agree, I will pull cards and discuss with my querent the reasons that they are not willing to consider the person in question. Sometimes people create unnecessary impediments to their happiness. It is important to figure out if that is happening, and to help the querent to realize it if it is.

If I see a known person of interest that seems like a good possibility for my querent, I may simply say "Don't be surprised if someone at work asks you out," or "The guy in the mailroom may have an interest in you."

The next question I ask is "Is my querent likely to meet anyone soon?" Again, I draw some cards and see what the future likely has in store. If romantic cards such as the Two of Cups, the Four of Wands, the Ten of Cups, the Ten of Pentacles or The Lovers show up I explore them, and work to make a prediction of the positive new relationship that is coming up.

If I see cards that are more negative, I try to see what is causing my querent to have such negative experiences in love.

Tarot Tour Guide

This flow chart graphically shows the process I use to help discern best steps and likely outcomes for a querent's romantic life.

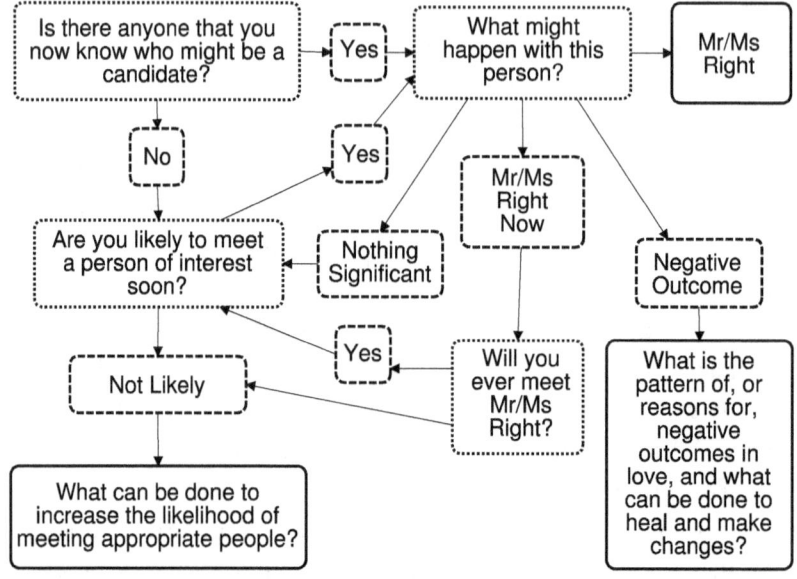

Figure 8 - Looking for Love Card Dialogue

Couples Readings

When I do a couples reading, I like to think that I am reading for three people. There's partner one, partner two, and the entity that they create as the couple. In a couple's reading I expect to discover information about each person's personal journey, about how they view each other and interact with each other, and about the nature of their shared journey.

Sample Reading-Still Single

Amber strode into my office as if she had been there many times before. She didn't wait to be invited into the reading room and acknowledged me only with a nod and a tight smile. I could tell that she spent more on perfume than I spent on my whole wardrobe. Her hair, make-up and clothes were impeccable. She wasn't old, but she wasn't as young as she was trying to appear.

I tried to engage her in small talk and told about the process we would follow in our reading. She smirked at everything I said, the only sound in the room was her airbrushed fingernails drumming on my table. Obviously, she was afraid to give anything away to me. She was a natural skeptic, perhaps visiting me on the advice of a friend.

I began the meditative breathing that I always use before and during a reading. I focused on finding the one thing that would knock her socks off, the one thing that she needed to hear. If I couldn't get her to open up her energy, she would get the unimpressive reading she was expecting.

Silently, I laid out the first spread, my usual eleven-card Celtic Cross. Sometimes I feel inspired to begin the reading with the very first card, the Significator. Here, the first card was the Five of Pentacles Reversed. Obviously, this woman needed, or had, some new opportunities. But I knew that my first sentence had to be really strong, so I kept my mouth shut and looked at the other cards.

More than half the cards in the spread were reversed. Hmm...This woman is not as sure of herself as she appears. That's why the expensive perfume and clothes. So many reversals might indicate, too, that she is not sure which direction to take. Still I say nothing, and the silence in the room grows thicker.

Few Major Arcana cards appear, only three. But the cards themselves, and their positions, are quite significant. The Moon appears as the client's Foundation, something from the past that she is built on, and carries with her. This could indicate that, for all her apparent skepticism, this woman could be deeply spiritual and quite possibly psychic herself. It could also, or additionally, be a reference to her family of origin, or her childhood. Perhaps there were some family mysteries, or she could have issues with her own sense of identity.

In the position of Recent Past is the Fool. For all that she seems very serious and subdued today, she does know how to have fun, she does know how to be silly, and she has had adventure in her life. Perhaps she has travelled recently or has embarked on some new experiences. All this information is helpful, but I still have no opening line.

I take stock of the eleven cards in front of me. Two reversed fives (Pentacles and Cups) are in prominent positions. She hopes to avoid strife and difficulty. The Tower is in the position of Hopes and Fears. Possibly she is waiting for something to go wrong, for the other shoe to drop.

I look for love and romance in her life and find none. No cards of the past, present or future indicate romantic love. In the position for Romance is the Seven of Pentacles Reversed. Does this mean that there has been a relationship that is no longer working? Or is it that there simply is not, and has not been, a relationship? Either way, it seems like this person is not happy with her love life as it now stands, and I tell her so.

Her smirk turns into a smile and then a laugh. I have passed her test, and now we can both enjoy the reading. She lets me know that she has been single for some time.

The Moon in her foundation position calls to me, and I say, "You seem to be looking for a true partner, not just someone to date." She nods, her eyes round. I continue "And yet you don't seem to have anyone around you who would be suitable, and you are afraid to trust people you don't know."

I'm on the right track now. This person needs faith in herself, in her ability to choose and trust a good partner, and to anticipate positive things in her life. I look again at the Tower in the position of Hopes and Fears.

The very deepest, darkest card is not addressing anything real, only the hopes and fears, the worries of her imagination. The Five of Cups Reversed in the Final Outcome Position sits next to the Tower and gives a significant piece of advice. It truly is all about attitude. Positive things will happen to this person when she expects positive things. I remember her attitude walking in to the reading and think this is probably the attitude she carries throughout her life; guarded, expecting the worst, unable to trust.

I see that she is tired, and without enthusiasm, as suggested by the Ace of Wands reversed in her Crown position. And yet she will have many options, as suggested by the Five of Pentacles reversed and the Four of Swords reversed.

The Five of Pentacles reversed is the Significator. This represents her need to "get her fair share" and the feeling that she might be missing opportunities. Since the only two Pentacles cards in the spread are reversed, I consider that she may not be happy with her job, career, or income. Overall, the eleven cards show a real lack of fun, motivation, energy, romance, and satisfaction.

In the position of Public Perception we see the Eight of Cups. Does she feel abandoned by the people around her, or separated from her loved ones? Perhaps she is just unable to reach out to other people. I tell her that I feel she has isolated herself from all types of love and relationships. She begins to cry.

Now the walls are down, and the reading is well underway. The Moon and the Fool represent her true ideals for herself. But they also represent her fears. She wants both the mystery and adventure of love, but she fears the unknown, and fears the risk. She is dissatisfied with all aspects of her life, although there is nothing terribly wrong with any part of her life. She is afraid of the future and doesn't know what to do to create the future that she wants.

So, what does she want? I pull a few cards. The Page of Cups suggests that she would like a family. The Eight of Pentacles tells me that she would like a job where she could learn new skills and be able to move up.

The Nine of Swords reversed suggests that perhaps anxiety and depression are a factor. She needs to simply feel better. I refer her to her physician for evaluation, suggesting that there might be a clinical problem of depression or anxiety. She tells me she has been wondering that as well and seems relieved that I have normalized it for her.

Then I pull the Kings of Wands. I suggest to her that her perfect partner would be creative, passionate, have a good sense of humor and a youthful outlook. She seems happy with that. I remind her that her attitude and her actions would dictate how quickly she achieved the things that she wanted in her life. I gently suggest that she sometimes lets her fear and insecurity create an atmosphere of aloofness, or coldness, around her. Of course, that makes it more difficult to meet people, either romantically or socially. She says that she is aware that she intimidates people but hadn't figured out why. She seems glad to have an understanding that it isn't that people don't like her, and that she can have some control over the way she is perceived. We agree that this has hurt her in the career realm as well.

In the end, she and I both felt that she had had a very positive and helpful reading. She felt empowered to make changes in her life and had a sense of how to do that. She was relieved when I told her that her worst problems were in her own fears and therefore controllable.

As she left my office, she was still a beautiful, well-put-together lady. But now she looked less like a solitary ice princess, and more like a person who felt capable of finding love.

Sample Reading: Single Again

Bob walks in wearing a baseball cap with a vulgar slogan embroidered on it. I wonder if he wore that hat specifically for me, or if he wears it all the time. He is a forty-ish athletic type.

I ignore the hat. I explain the procedure of the reading in a professional tone and begin laying out the cards. First card out, in the Significator position, is the Eight of Swords Reversed. The card is screaming at me, so I put the deck down, make eye contact with Bob, and say "You are being freed from something that has been holding you down." He nods his head and says nothing.

Next card, in the atmosphere position, is the Three of Wands. "You need to be thinking about your future and making plans toward your future success." Thinking about the two cards combined, I say "It is likely that the future you had originally planned for yourself has changed considerably. What you had expected will not happen, and the future is now open. Do not grieve the future that was lost, celebrate what can now be." He nods again, with a half-smile, and sheepishly takes off the stupid hat.

The Challenge card is the Nine of Pentacles. The woman on the card seems to be smiling smugly, more than usual. I'm ready to discover what it is that Bob is freeing himself from, what it is that has changed his view of the future so drastically. Logic would say that it is either a change in job or relationship. The Pentacles card as the Challenge might indeed indicate a job issue. But I am so very aware of the smug smile of the woman on the card. It must be a relationship issue, perhaps one that is raising a financial concern.

Only three cards into the spread, I am ready to take a stab at the heart of the matter. "Are you going through a divorce or a break-up?" I ask. He nods. "My wife just served me with papers." He says it in a sorrowful voice. Looking back at the Eight of Swords Reversed, I suggest to him that maybe, as painful as it is, this is a good thing. He nods thoughtfully.

I focus back on the Challenge card, the Nine of Pentacles. Privately, I'm thinking that his wife has perhaps outgrown him. But I'm not going to say that. It also seems that he may be getting ready to take a financial loss in this divorce. I remain silent as I look at the other cards.

His Foundation card is the Tower reversed. "I'm not sure that this marriage has ever gone really well." I say. The Five of Cups falls into Events of the Recent Past. Probably both husband and wife are guilty of focusing on the negative, maybe even blaming each other for things that didn't go the right way. I suggest that such a blame-fest has been going on for years, and he smiles. The Crown card is The Chariot. That's hopeful. I suggest to him that he is able to master any circumstance, and to move on and be successful. I also ask him if he has, or is thinking of buying, a hot sports car. When this is all over, he tells me, he's getting a Mustang. "Good for you," I tell him, "you should be able to do so, but you might consider buying it used. This divorce will have you pinching your pennies for a while."

In the Near Future position is the Queen of Swords Reversed. Bob may suspect his soon-to-be-ex of dishonesty. Truthfully, he should probably be aware that she is not a bastion of integrity. This card along with the Nine of Pentacles as a Challenge card suggest that Bob's wife will make a play for as much money as she can get from him, whether she deserves it or not. She is likely to go to dishonest measures if she needs to.

She may also be actively working to get their mutual friends and family on her side. In the Public Perception position is Strength Reversed. Bob's friends and family see him as angry and perhaps violent. Is that really his character, or is that just what she wants people to think?

I decide to be straightforward with him and tell him all that I see here. He admits to having a temper but feels that it has been blown out of proportion and does indeed suspect his wife of a great deal of dishonesty.

In the position of Relationships is the Hierophant. What an interesting card. All at once, it suggests that Bob had hoped to have a traditional and life-long marriage, that he truly needs a good attorney, and that his wife will try to portray him as controlling. Bob agrees with all of this.

I suggest to Bob that he needs to trust in his attorney rather than in his own feelings. I suggest that his wife may feel that he was trying to control her, or oppress her, and that she wants to be in her own power now. Bob snorts sarcastically.

Honestly, I think I would not like to be married to Bob either, but of course I don't mention that. My job is to help him get through this difficult time and give him some perspective. So far, so good.

In the position of Hopes and Fears is The Devil. At this point I figure Bob trusts me, and so I ask if drugs or alcohol has been an issue in the marriage. Yes, he tells me. He likes to drink, and his wife doesn't like it. I ask if he considers himself a problem drinker. He tells me he's not sure. I take his hand that lies on the table next to the cards and I gently tell him that, as he goes through this difficult time, part of what he will need to do is to focus on building a new life for himself, a better life. Whatever wrong he did in the marriage, and whatever wrong she did, won't matter in the long run. What will matter are his decisions going forward. And some of those decisions will be about how he takes care of himself. I suggest that he is a guy who likes to have fun, but he is also a guy who likes to be in control of a situation, and a guy with a bit of a temper. The way I say it doesn't seem to bother him, he nods and agrees with me. I tell him that I think he really needs to look long and hard at his drinking, and at the very least not let his new single status contribute to the problem. Then I take a breath and say something that is crude and tough, but also true. "Your marriage might have survived you being a control freak and you having a few drinks, and it might have survived your wife being a bitch and being a little unwilling to see and speak the truth. But there's no way it was going to survive all of that at once!"

He sits silent for a moment, and then he laughs for a long time. "I came here to see if I could save my relationship," he said. "But I have been fooling myself for a long time." "Well," I said gently, "It does seem like the two of you have brought out the worst in each other for a long time. It would be good if you could find someone who could show you their best and bring out the best in you."

In the Final Outcome position is The King of Cups. I tell Bob that he will love again, that he will heal from this difficulty and that all will be well for him in the future. I remind him that he is a sensitive person, and that this has been very hurtful and stressful for him. I reassure him that this difficulty will not go on forever; that someday it will all be in the past.

Now all the cards are laid out, I take stock of the big picture. Five Major Arcana cards in the spread indicate the life-changing nature of Bob's present circumstances. Only one Pentacle card, and that in the Challenge position, indicates that money will be an issue. The Three of Wands, Eight of Swords reversed, Chariot and the King of Cups all speak to a happier future for Bob.

But many questions are unanswered. There was nothing in the opening spread about children or career. And there is only a hint about future love in the King of Cups. I'm not quite sure why Bob's wife is filing for divorce or how they both feel about it. I get the sense that the marriage has been rocky for a while and that control may be an issue. I have the basic story, now I need to fill in the details.

I pick up all the cards and shuffle them a few times. First, I am interested in his immediate family situation. Does he have children? Are they a factor in the divorce? I pull a few cards. I get the Eight of Wands, the Tower, The Fool Reversed and the Seven of Wands. None of these cards are specifically cards that speak to children. They certainly do speak to change, stress, the need to defend oneself, and immaturity. If he does have kids, he probably won't have custody of them. There is so much difficulty and trauma here that I assume kids are involved. "You have kids?" I say to him, half as a statement and half as a question.

"Yeah" he says.

"They'll stay with their mother." I say, "and she'll want to turn them against you."

"It's already happening," he says. So what kind of father is he, I wonder. Silently, I pull a few cards to answer that question. Four of Cups, and Seven of Pentacles reversed. Apparently, he is too lazy and childish himself to be a good father. I'd divorce him, too! But how do I present that to him in a positive way?

"You and your wife haven't been on the same page for a long time," I say. "Her wants and needs are different from your wants and needs. I know that she expects the worst from you, but show her that you can be a good guy and be cooperative in the process. That way it will be over quickly and easily."

Of course, Bob wants to know just how easy that will be. How will the divorce go? I pull one card, The Queen of Pentacles. Bob should probably get used to writing her checks and recognize that she is a good mother to his children. If Bob is willing to send the checks on time, the divorce should go smoothly. Of course, I remind Bob to work with his attorney throughout the process.

Now he wants to know about future love relationships. Judging from his marriage, he would be better not to look for anything serious right now. Gently I tell him that it seems that he's more interested in fun than commitment right now. That's one of the reasons his marriage has failed. It's likely that other relationships would fail for the same reasons.

I draw four cards again, Judgment, the Knight of Wands, Strength Reversed and the Eight of Pentacles. Judgment suggests that, until he has closure with his marriage, he will stay single. The Knight of Wands suggests that he will pursue enjoyment and recreation. Strength Reversed reveals the anger that he is feeling. The Eight of Pentacles suggests that his focus should be work and career, and that he should pursue learning and advancement within his profession at this time.

Bob nods his head thoughtfully. "I was hoping for a new girlfriend to help me forget all this." He says. "But I see now that I should take care of myself first, and wait until I have something to bring to the table before I get myself involved with someone."

And with that, it occurs to me that maybe one day Bob will be able to become a good husband to someone.

Tarot as a Tool for Heart-to-Heart Communication

While communication is certainly an attribute of the element of Air, communication from the heart can be associated with Water. The trick is to get out of the Air and into the Water, or out of your mind and into your heart.

Even very effective communicators can find it a struggle to honestly and accurately communicate their feelings. Tarot is a great tool in assisting you to understand your feelings, and the best way to communicate them so they can be easily understood. Tarot can also help you hear someone else, even if their message is unclear, confusing, or hurtful.

If a love of tarot is something that you share with your partner, your communication together is automatically easier because you can use the images to describe your feelings and know that you will be understood.

If you are conducting a reading for someone, it may be part of your job to help your client understand what is in their heart, and how to communicate it. Likewise, you may have to use the cards to help clients understand what is in the heart of someone with whom they are trying to communicate.

Tarot is a wonderful tool for personal introspection. If you know you need to have a difficult conversation with someone, take a few minutes with the cards first.

Center and ground yourself. Ask meaningful questions in dialogue with the cards.

How do I really feel about this situation?

What do I need to communicate to this person?

How is my communication likely to be received?

What do I need to do to ensure a positive experience?

What are my goals for this communication?

Those are but a few questions that might be helpful in preparing for important heart-to-heat communication. It is important to use the cards to help you understand your less-than-positive feelings and reactions, as well as those of the person with whom you'll be communicating.

In heart-to-heart communication, your goal must always be to find the highest ground and serve the highest good. It's important to acknowledge, however, that you may harbor feelings that do not serve your highest good. The tarot can help you understand those feelings and find a way to honor them that doesn't use them as an inappropriate basis for important decisions within your relationship.

There are many cards that speak directly about communication, and many more that may caution us about ways in which we should, or should not, communicate. The suit of Swords, of course, is the traditional suit of communication, while Cups is the suit of the heart. The Page of Cups represents honest and loving communication from the heart. The Ace of Swords, of course, represents a new truth, or a need for honest communication. The Three of Swords represents the anguish of heartache, often the product of difficult communication.

Sometimes, we react to communication in a defensive way. The Seven of Wands or the Nine of Wands might indicate defensiveness. The Two of Cups might indicate loving communication between two people. The Two of Wands might discuss communicating a vision for the future, while the Ace of Wands might discuss communicating a creative idea, an inspiring idea, or even some explosive anger! The Four and Five of Cups might suggest a negative or immature attitude. The Four of Pentacles might suggest a person who is reluctant to share their feelings.

Cards might discuss the best place to have a meaningful conversation, such as at home (Ten of Pentacles), in a quiet, neutral place (Four of Swords), in the car (Chariot) or at work (Three of Pentacles).

If you have had a misunderstanding or miscommunication with someone, you can use the cards to help discern what the person is really thinking and feeling, and the best ways to re-open the doors of communication.

Playing with the tarot cards during communication can be helpful whether or not the person with whom you are communicating is conversant in tarot. You can both look through the deck and find cards that represent how you feel. You can talk about the images and how the images describe your feelings. You can draw cards at random and see what bearing they have on the situation. This can be a great ice-breaker, and a way to get a difficult conversation underway.

You may be asked to use the cards to facilitate communication between people.

It is interesting to have them each draw one card at random that will describe what each of them are really feeling. Then have them draw another to show what it is that they most want to communicate to the other person. Your skillful interpretation is critical, so ask them to be honest in reporting what resonates for them as truth, and what doesn't.

They say that a picture is worth a thousand words. Sometimes the right picture can help you find the few words that are exactly right.

Tarot and the Intuitive Process

Intuition is often described as a "feeling." Since we associate the element of Water with feelings, it makes sense that we associate Water with intuition. Intuition is evoked by the flowing nature of water, along with its depth, its strength, and its mystery.

Working with the tarot will help you to be more intuitive and will help you to more easily trust your intuition. Simply being in contact with the tarot images helps you to open pathways and make the connections that allow intuition to flow. Using the cards in divination to confirm your intuitive feelings will give you confidence.

Using intuition in the interpretation of tarot is critical to giving precise and informative tarot readings. There is one question that new tarot students always ask. "How can I tell how I should interpret a card, since there are so many interpretations possible?" It is true, for instance, that the Ace of Pentacles could be either a new job or a new baby. Most students will quickly understand that interpretations are based on combining the cards. In our example of the Ace of Pentacles, we might assume a pregnancy if it came up with the Empress or a new job if it came up with the Three of Pentacles. Every great tarot reader knows to look for these kinds of combinations, but also knows that intuition plays a strong and largely unteachable role in accurate card interpretation.

We also meet tarot readers, even professionals, who do not have a standard or traditional understanding of tarot interpretation at all. They use the tarot solely as an intuitive tool.

To use the tarot intuitively, simply allow yourself to monitor what you feel, think or remember when you look at the card images. What do you notice in the pictures? Are you drawn to the colors, the numbers, or the facial expressions? What about the flowers, or the animals?

Once, when doing a reading, I was asked about a family member who had recently died. I don't remember what card I pulled, or what deck I was reading. In the background of the card I pulled were some pumpkins. When I saw the card, even though I knew well its meaning, and there were many things to look at in the picture, all I could see were the pumpkins. I told the querent that I could say nothing but "Pumpkin." She started to cry. "Pumpkin" was the nickname by which this family member was known. In this case, I used my intuition to guide me to the part of the picture I needed to see, and then to say exactly what I saw.

Sometimes being intuitive means using your psychic ability to flesh out the story that you see in the cards. Sometimes it means gauging your client's reaction to something, to see if the client is telling the truth, or open to hearing a deeper level of truth. Sometimes it means being guided to pay attention to one card more than another, or to ask specific questions of the cards.

In a tarot reading, intuition is often aided by the invocation of spirit, in the form of an opening meditation or prayer. Remember that intuition is the twin sister of imagination. Be willing to let your imagination run a little bit. By imagining possibilities for your client, you will be able to intuit probabilities.

Tarot cards that specifically speak to the intuitive process include the Moon, the High Priestess, the Seven of Cups, the Queen of Cups, the Queen of Wands, and the Queen of Pentacles. Traditionally, intuition is considered the domain of women, and an aspect of femininity. The feminine suits and cards are more likely to speak of intuition than are the more active, masculine cards. This by no means suggests that men can't be intuitive; it simply means that both men and women need to tap into their receptive nature to be truly intuitive.

The best tarot readings are both intuitive and interpretive. By using both methods at once we allow the cards to supply us with the best and richest information possible.

Tarot and the End of a Relationship

People often seek tarot readings when considering the end of a relationship or as they struggle for healing after the relationship has ended. Sometimes a tarot reading reveals the end of the relationship before the client is quite ready to hear it!

The tarot also offers wisdom for lovers at all stages of relationships. For instance, Major Arcana six, The Lovers, is related to the element of Air. One might have assumed it would have been Water, as Water relates to love and emotion. As a card of Air, it advises integrity, communication, and most importantly, discernment. These qualities of Air are essential for choosing wisely in love. When we don't choose wisely, the pain we feel will often be reflected by the suit of Air, Swords.

The suit of Cups, ace through ten, offers advice and comment on different stages of relationships. The Cups Court shows the skills that are needed to form and maintain healthy relationships.

When we look at the ace through ten of Cups, we can see a journey that begins with the heart overflowing with love in the ace, followed by the forming of a partnership, in the two, and the celebration of that partnership, in the three. But trouble soon comes in the four, when we question our choices, or find that we aren't happy, or stay stuck in a negative attitude. The question in the Four of Cups is whether it is the relationship or the attitude that is negative.

In the Five of Cups we see loss, sadness and, disappointment. But if we turn to see the cups that are not spilt, we see two full cups standing undisturbed. In the face of a lost relationship, those two standing cups may evoke the Two of Cups and remind us that a more perfect relationship may await us in the future. If the Five of Cups references problems within a loving relationship, those two standing cups may serve to direct attention to that which is most important; the love that exists in the relationship.

The Six of Cups causes us to look to our past. It could suggest that we are bringing issues from childhood, or from a past relationship, into our current relationship. It also suggests a reason that unhealthy relationships persist. Often, when I ask the cards why a client is staying in an obliviously unhealthy relationship, the answer is the Six of Cups. They honor the history of the relationship. When you ask them why they perpetuate the relationship they often say, "well, we've been together for a long time." On a spiritual level, the Six of Cups could suggest some past life karma between the couple as well. Privately, I often think that this card is saying that the relationship has a past, but not a future. It is also true, though, that it could remind a loving couple to return to the passion and vision they had in the beginning of their relationship.

The Seven of Cups can indicate some confusion in a relationship. What do you really want, and what do you really feel?

The Eight of Cups can discuss evaluating your emotions and letting go of those that hold you back. This could involve walking away, either from negative emotions or from the relationship itself.

With the Nine and Ten of Cups we see the satisfaction, happiness and contentment that can come from a loving relationship.

Stories from the Suit of Cups

Three sisters came to see me for readings. They all sat together and commented on each other's readings and on the tarot images. One of them notices that in each person's spread, the Three of Cups was in a prominent position. "Oh my gosh!" She said. "Look, it's three women, just like us! This is a picture of us!"

Over and over, for more than a year, I kept drawing the Six of Cups for myself. I couldn't understand what it meant. At a Tarot Circle meeting the conversation turned to cards that come up repeatedly and what they might mean. I shared my Six of Cups and said that I didn't have a clue what it meant. "Spend time with your mother," someone said. "Go back to your childhood home."

I took the advice and called my mother to arrange a visit. Just a few months later she was diagnosed with cancer. As a result, I returned to the house of my childhood to live.

Tarot Magick for Love and Healing

This magick works directly with the heart center, also known as the fourth chakra. The idea is to heal the heart and prepare it to welcome true love.

I like to do this magick with candles. Since the magick is most effective if you let the candles burn out, choose small candles with a short burning time. Choose one green candle to represent the heart chakra, one blue to represent healing energy, one red for vitality and passion, and one pink for love and romance.

Place the green candle in the center, and the other candles around it. Place the Ace of Cups near the green candle, the Star near the blue candle, the Ace of Wands near the red candle, and the Two of Cups near the pink candle.

Create your sacred space, breathe, ground, center, and focus.

Focus on your heart and breathe into it. Take the Ace of Cups, hold it to your heart and say:

May my heart open and heal. May I be ready to give and receive love abundantly.

Place the Ace of Cups back in its place near the green candle, and light the candle.

Now take the Star, hold it to your heart, and say:

May healing flow through me, and bring me peace, balance, and wellness.

Place the Star back in its place near the blue candle, and light the candle.

Now Take the Ace of Wands, hold it to your heart and say:

I am alive, awake and aware. My energy is a beacon that will attract love to me.

Place the Ace of Wands near the red candle, and light it.

Finally, hold the Two of Cups to your heart and say:

I am loving and capable, and I draw to myself one who is available, compatible and ready for an honest and fulfilling relationship.

Place the Two of Cups near the pink candle and light the candle.

Sit with the candles and meditate, write or work with your tarot cards until the candles are burned out. Leave the cards with the candles while the candles burn.

Once the candles burn out, shuffle the cards back into your deck.

May the element of Water bless you on your journey.

CHAPTER ELEVEN

The Element of Fire- Passion, Creativity, Vitality and Spirituality.

This chapter is dedicated to the element of Fire. We will discuss ways of using tarot to inspire our creativity, pursue our passions and connect with our spirituality.

Fire, perhaps more than any of the other elements, has a place in spiritual and community rituals and observances in most, if not all, cultures.

Most churches use candles on their altars. Wedding ceremonies can include the lighting of the "Unity Candle." In many cultures fire is used to return our dead loved ones to the Earth.

Our family rituals often involve gathering around the fireplace for winter holidays, singing and toasting marshmallows around a campfire for summer holidays, and of course, celebrating birthdays with candles on a cake.

Even misguided religious zealots would rather burn books than simply throw them away. Those schooled in magickal work know that committing something to the fire can be a way of releasing it.

The carrying of the Olympic torch and the eternal flame at the Tomb of the Unknown Soldier are other examples of our multicultural understanding of the sacred nature of fire.

Symbolically, we use the image of fire to confer the ideas of both purification and tribulation. We talk about "trial by fire," and making it "through the fire." We also talk about holding someone's "feet to the fire."

We also speak of the fires of passion, be they sexual, creative, or violent. Fire can be a metaphor for both sex and anger. Saying "I burn for you" is very different than saying "You really burn me up." One conveys sexual attraction, the other anger. When we "play with fire", we are invoking something that is both tantalizing and dangerous.

Fire also represents the kundalini energy as it rises, like a snake, through the chakras. In many cultures, Fire is associated with reptiles, from fire-breathing dragons to snakes to the salamanders that adorn many tarot Wands cards.

Some depictions of the fiery tarot wands show them not with flames, but with new green life sprouting. The living, or blooming, wand is often used as a tool for the element of Fire in magickal traditions. Here we can clearly see that Fire is representative of the life force itself, the chi energy within all living things.

Navigating the metaphysical path of Fire in our lives can be tricky. Too much Fire and we are lost in our own passions. Too little and we lack the vitality we need to be at our best. Tarot can help us find our inspiration, temper our anger, nurture our vitality, and explore our sexuality.

Interestingly, as much as fire itself is a cultural and spiritual symbol, its attributes, sexuality and conflict, are society's evil stepchildren. As we own our fiery nature, we can learn to honor our sexual nature and our warrior nature in ways that are healing and helpful. As with all the elements, finding the right balance is the key.

Fire inspires us and teaches us to create. Fire connects us to spirit and represents the eternal and magnificent part of us which is spirit. Fire motivates us, purifies us, and tests us.

Meditation, yoga, dance, martial arts, and athletics are all tools to help us balance our Fire energy. Just as with a hearth fire, our internal spiritual Fire needs to be nurtured and controlled, stoked, and tempered. Introspection with tarot helps us to find tools and set limits and goals.

Tarot magick can be used to summon energy, inspiration, strength, wisdom and spiritual connection.

We call on Fire to make us better and stronger. We channel Fire as we create, protect, and defend. Fire is the spiritual force that serves to ignite within us the joys of being human. We use tarot to help us understand and balance that force.

Invocation of Fire

The Ace of Wands is a magickal tool that invokes Fire. Through this invocation, we bring the energy of Fire to us, and we dedicate the tarot as a tool that will help us to ignite our passions, inspire our creativity, heal our anger, defend our boundaries and connect with the eternal spiritual life force. We will find inspiration for our projects and a sense of balance and purpose for ourselves. We will find the ability to connect with spirit in meditation, movement, art, dedication, and divination. As we connect ourselves with Fire, we avail ourselves of its purifying and energizing nature.

Look at your Ace of Wands. See it as the core symbol of life waiting to happen, unlimited energy and divinely channeled creativity. Stand up. Hold the Ace of Wands to your heart. Take a deep breath and visualize yourself standing by a blazing bonfire on a cool evening. Think about the flames, the smoke, the heat, and the crackling of the wood as it is consumed. Raise your arms and feel the force of the fire push against of body as you begin to dance with the flames. Say an invocation, such as the following:

"As I connect myself to Fire, I bring Fire to my spirit. With this wand I bring passion, creativity, excitement and energy to my life. I honor tarot as a tool of Fire that will help me to understand the power of creation, and my own ability to create without limitation. I dedicate my tarot cards as a tool that will help me to know passion and express passion to the world around me.

With this wand and with my entire being, I call on the powers of Fire. May it purify me, strengthen me, and make me an exciting expression of creative and spiritual energy that will offer warmth, light, laughter, healing and inspiration to all the world around me."

Wands Fire Exercise

Look at the Wands cards two through ten. Each of these cards represents some aspect of the creative process. Look at each card and think about how creativity is portrayed in each one.

From the Wands two through ten, choose the cards that represent where you feel you are right now in your journey toward embracing and enacting your creativity fully.

Now look at the cards you didn't choose. From them, choose the ones that you would like to set as goals for your further progress. Now look at the remaining cards, those that you didn't choose. Do any of these represent aspects of your past, or attitudes that you would like to avoid on your journey of creative and passionate discovery?

Major Arcana Fire Exercise

Place the Major Arcana cards that are traditionally associated with the element of Fire in front of you. They are the Emperor, Strength, Wheel of Fortune, Temperance, the Tower, the Sun, and Judgment. Think about these cards in association with the element of Fire. You may have noticed that there are more Major Arcana cards associated with Fire than with the other elements. Why do you think that is?

In what way does each of these cards symbolize the element of Fire?

What do you learn about Fire when you look at these cards?

What do you learn about each of these cards when you think of it as a symbol of Fire?

Clues for the Beginner- Having Fun

One aspect of Fire that we sometimes forget is fun. Fire relates to our recreation, our humor, our competitive athletics, and our play. And, while tarot is a serious book of spiritual wisdom, it is also a game.

Most tarot artists include some images that are funny; perhaps even clever jokes for the observant reader. Consider the snail in the

Waite Nine of Pentacles, for instance, or the general goofiness of the Knight of Wands from the same deck.

It is also true that the best tarot readers are able to use humor in their readings and make the experience fun.

As often misunderstood spiritual people, tarot readers are sometimes guilty of taking themselves a little too seriously. Avoid this by enjoying funny images in your tarot deck. When you interpret the cards, look for synchronicities that are humorous as well as profound. Make up games to play with the cards, on your own and with your tarot friends.

Tarot and the Creative Process

More and more, tarot is being used, explored and accepted as a serious creative device. Corrine Kenner's book, *Tarot for Writers*, suggests that writers adopt tarot as a tool to help them in their process. Based in part on this book and its success, writers' groups for tarot readers are sprouting up all over the world.

Meanwhile, there are a significant number of new tarot decks published each year worldwide. Tarot art inspires people to create more tarot art, and thus new decks are born.

Tarot collage has become an important exercise for many tarot students. Tarot groups often hold tarot-themed dinners complete with tarot costumes.

In serious ways and in silly ways, tarot can help us explore, nurture, and guide our creative process.

The suit of Wands is an interesting expression of creative struggle, and the journey of the artist. We start with the inspiration in the Ace of Wands, move into the planning stages with the two, and with the three we see our first success, celebrated and made manifest in the four. With the five we see the struggle for growth, but with the six, recognition and success. The seven suggests ideas or projects that need defending, and might feel overwhelming. You might need to multi-task to complete your projects. The eight suggests creative energy that has a life of its own. The nine speaks of a need for patience, a need to heal and a need to protect both yourself and your project. The ten speaks of the long labor of love of which only the artist is capable. The vision of the completed work sustains the heavy burdens that still must be carried.

The discussion of creativity is not limited to the suit of Wands, however. Temperance is often called the card of "art." The Magician possesses the tools and skills to create whatever he would like. Both the Three and Eight of Pentacles can express creative work. A best-case interpretation for the Seven of Swords can be "crafty solutions." Tarot is always ready to help you tap into your own creative source.

There are many practical ways to use tarot to stimulate creativity. Whatever your media or project, it is always appropriate to ask, "Where shall I go next?" and pull a card. Or, "How will this character react?" Or, "What colors shall I use in my painting?" Or even, "What should the subject of my next song be?"

A nice way of stimulating creativity and studying tarot is to choose a tarot card to illustrate in collage or in photography. But why stop with two dimensions? There is something about tarot that makes us want to express its energy in many ways. There are tarot songs, tarot topiaries, tarot jigsaw puzzles, tarot sculptures, and tarot poetry. Let tarot wake up your creativity as you study it! Use it with a familiar medium or as a way of exploring a new medium!

As an example, here is a tarot poem I wrote about the Tower, one of the Major Arcana Fire cards.

The Tower

Yielding only to flame and destiny
And rendered into dust
The Tower crumbles and begins to fall.
The fullness of its destruction is inevitable.
Torn, falling, brick by brick, and wall by wall.

Is this a metaphor for some internal shadow journey?
Or a dark harbinger of doom, or worse?
Dread curls around your spine
And laughs as you relinquish hope
Abandoned, injured, the weight of flesh a curse.

Pray you learned well the Fool's lesson
To leap, with faith, in good time.
Flawed foundations rock; ominous, frightening
Welcome the collapse
Raining droplets of Spirit and dirt.
No fear in the storm
Raging, releasing, enlightening.

Solid stone stands no more
Yet burned and broken flesh is strangely
Crawling, quivering, shaking, quite alive.
Ashes swept away reveal new ground, new hope,
Something shining.
The victory is simply to survive.

The Sexual Tarot

It would be impossible to look at the Ace of Wands and not see a phallic symbol, or to consider the many aspects of the High Priestess without including her virginal nature. Because tarot speaks to all of life, it speaks especially to our prime biological directive— reproduction.

Of course, sexuality is so much more than continuation of the species. It is creative expression, a way of sharing energy in relationship, a way of raising energy for magickal purposes, a way of honoring our sacred humanity, and a way of connecting with the Divine.

Many clients and readers turn to tarot to calm their anxieties around sexual issues. Practitioners of sex magick may use tarot in ritual.

Whether reading for yourself or others, sexual issues will make themselves known in the cards, whether or not the questions are asked. A few cards have clear sexual meaning for me; you may discover others. It is important to remember that these meanings are appropriate some of the time, not all the time.

Some of the Major Arcana cards that can be sexual references include the Magician, which could indicate the need to try some new technique, especially in the use of toys. The High Priestess, of course, represents abstinence from sex. When she is reversed, she could represent a feeling of guilt for sexual conduct, whether deserved or not. The Empress, as a pregnant woman, could be a warning to use good birth control protocol. The Devil can represent unhealthy relationships, but it could also represent BDSM-style play. The Star can represent a phenomenal sexual attraction or experience.

In the Minor Arcana, the Ace of Wands is the erect penis, indicative of sexual desire. When reversed, the attraction may no longer be there, or erectile dysfunction may be an issue. The Eight of Swords may indicate bondage-play, while the Three of Cups may indicate a woman who prefers women, or may indicate polyamorous relationships.

There are some lessons in sexual relations inherent in tarot. Most significant to me is a study of the Ace of Cups and the Ace of Wands. If the Ace of Wands is about male sexual desire, then we could certainly say that the Ace of Cups could indicate female sexual desire. But that would mean that for women, sexual desire is a thing of the heart, while with men, it is a thing of the penis. So often that turns out to be true!

Some tarot enthusiasts use the cards as a tool for play in sacred relationship. One way to do this is to simply pull a card and let it tell you what to do next. Use your imagination as you let the images, keywords and traditional interpretations take on new, suggestive meanings.

Tarot can also be used as a tool for communication within a relationship, especially around topics than can sometimes be difficult to discuss. For instance, if there is a particular concern that you have, but are uncomfortable sharing, you might prepare yourself for the conversation by dialoguing with the cards. Use the cards to explore your true feelings. You will find ways to present those feelings so they can be heard in a loving way.

An intimate couple might use cards drawn at random to help them relate their feelings or concerns. They might also take turns choosing cards cognitively whose images represent their feelings, or their hopes, or their fears within the relationship.

Tarot can supply a common language of images along with the ability to create a connection with spirit. You can be playful, profound and passionate as you explore tarot as a tool in the exploration and understanding of human sexuality.

Tarot and Divination

Many psychic tools or methods can be used for divination. Like runes and other oracle cards, tarot is a tool of random token divination. I have always believed random itself to be a thing of magick; a spiritual force that gives the universe room to work.

Not all forms of divination include random as part of their process. All divination methods involve interpretation, be it the lines of the palms, the arrangement of the tea leaves, or the symbols on the cards. Tarot is unique in the way that it is reimagined by multiple artists over time. Another thing that makes tarot unique is its structure, and its correspondences to so many occult systems.

Some people see the tarot only as a tool of divination. They ignore its functions as a tool of meditation, creativity, magick, and spiritual growth. Mostly, I think this happens because tarot is such a very good tool of divination.

The question is, of course, what leads us to pick a specific card? When the cards are randomly mixed, does our Higher Self know which cards we need to see, and psychically know which card is which? Do higher spiritual forces manipulate the cards being drawn?

Each reader has his or her own beliefs about how and why card divination is so effective.

There is an important rule to know about divination that applies to much in life. What you get out of it depends on what you put into it. A quick, casual look at the cards may be helpful, but will not give as deep or profound an answer as you will get from a more focused divination session.

What makes a focused divination session? Part of it is mindset. Tarot cards can be enjoyed with wine and friends and will provide an evening's entertainment. But a reading that is conducted in sacred space is likely to provide more insight and inspiration. That tarot works in all atmospheres is another testament to its versatility and usefulness.

To get the most out of tarot divination, remember these important points.

- Perform your reading in a comfortable space.
- Create sacred space with ritual, prayer, or meditation.
- Allot enough time to conduct your reading.
- Ask questions directly of Spirit (angels, deities, guides, loved ones, etc.) as you pull the cards.

Whenever and wherever you choose to perform divination, consider this: tarot divination works startlingly well when you don't think about it too much. Simply pull a card, look at it, and say what comes to mind. Tarot divination is equally impressive when you think deeply about it. Do that by meditating on the card, by deconstructing the image, or by seeing just how many meanings you can think of for a specific card.

The element of Fire is the element of inspiration. Whether it comes from a stream of consciousness flash or from deep meditation, that inspiration is the source of true communication with the Divine.

Tarot as a Tool for Psychic Development

Not only is tarot a tool of psychics, it is a tool that will make you more psychic as you use it. This process will happen whether or not you think about it or focus on it. The cards, by design, will heighten psychic awareness over time.

The question is, how does this happen? The first answer is simply that it is a function of practice. As in anything else, the more you do something the better you become at it. The next answers are more mystical. It may be that, since tarot is very visual, working with them opens the third eye; the brow chakra that controls eyesight, imagination, and psychic vision. It may be that viewing sacred images directly affects us on a very deep, or very expansive, level.

I believe that most people do possess some psychic talent. I wish that our society could acknowledge psychic ability as a basic, normal human talent. Then we could train kids for it the way we do with other talents like music or sports. The result, I believe, would be far-reaching. Not only would we all be more intuitive and able to make better decisions, we would be much more emotionally healthy, overall. I believe that suppression or neglect of intuitive and psychic abilities can result in depression, anxiety, and a host of other emotional issues. The acknowledgement and utilization of psychic ability, on the other hand, can be empowering, and healing.

Like most talents, psychic ability can be developed, and improved. Working with tarot is a good first step toward psychic development.

Another seemingly obvious step is this. Simply pay attention! Pay attention to things you notice around you. Sometimes the universe speaks to us in signs. Look for animals, plants, clouds—anything that strikes you as important. Pay attention to synchronicities. When you hear the same word, phrase or concept multiple times, it's probably important. Pay attention to your feelings. Sometimes it's hard to separate anxiety from intuition. I tell my students that anxiety is the voice that screams, while intuition is the whisper you must listen to hear.

Some specific tarot cards refer to psychic development. When they come up in a reading they may indicate the psychic abilities of your client. They may come up to focus you on your own psychic development. You could also use these cards to manifest greater psychic abilities through tarot magick.

I see Judgment as hearing the voice of the angels. Therefore, it could refer to channeling, or communication with those who have passed on. The Moon can be a card of psychic knowledge, but also warns us to be careful to discern what is real. The High Priestess speaks of the true psychic wisdom and power found in meditation and the study of sacred texts. The Hermit speaks of the pilgrimage of the seeker and the need for deep introspection to discover truth. The Ace of Wands can indicate a lightning bolt of inspiration, while the Tower can represent the enlightenment that destroys outmoded thinking and beliefs.

Tarot and Dreams

When we think of dreams, we think of two different things. There are the dreams we have when we are asleep. We also refer to our aspirations and hopes for the future as dreams. Tarot relates to both types of dreams.

Tarot communicates information from our subconscious mind to our conscious mind. Sometimes, our sleeping dreams do the same thing. Like tarot cards, dreams can be interpreted to reveal helpful information. Some people believe that our dreams are sent to us by our guardians in spirit, just as people believe that those guardians speak to us through tarot.

Tarot can be used to interpret dreams. Most simply, you can ask "What does this dream mean?" and pull a few cards. You can also design a spread for the specific dream. Think about the different symbols, people and events in the dream, and create a position to help you interpret each one. When you interpret the spread, you will see how each aspect of the dream relates to your life.

Tarot can also help us understand and achieve our dreams for the future. Many tarot spreads include a position for hopes or goals. Some of the best readings come from asking the question "What do I need to do to manifest my dreams and goals?"

As we incorporate tarot into our lives, it often enters our sleeping dreams. I advise my new tarot students to sleep with their tarot deck under their pillow. They often report that the cards show up in their dreams. For many, this is the real beginning of their deep relationship with tarot.

Since tarot is a language of the subconscious, the subconscious will use it to communicate with us in dreams. Once, I had snapped at a colleague inappropriately. That night, my dream was simply one huge tarot card. That card was "Strength." The message was that I needed to tame the savage beast of my own anger. Since it was a tarot colleague, I shared my dream with her by way of apology the next day. She appreciated it as much as I did.

Sometimes tarot enters the dreams of those for whom we read. I had a telephone client whom I had never met in person. She had no knowledge of tarot other than receiving readings from time to time. She reported to me a fascinating dream, in which I was reading for her in person.

In the dream, I handed her a piece of paper with the number twenty-one on it. I told her that everything she wanted was coming to her, if she could just be patient.

My client had no idea that tarot cards were numbered. She couldn't have known that card twenty-one, the World, could be an indicator of one's ultimate future success.

In the reading that I gave her after she told me of the dream, the World did figure prominently, and the interpretation was the same.

I see a few cards as referring to both kinds of dreams. The Moon can say "Pay attention to your dreams!" meaning that, in sleep, important messages will be given. The Nine of Swords can speak of nightmares. The Seven of Cups can speak both of our sleeping dreams and our hopes for the future. The Two of Wands is about manifesting our dreams for the future. The High Priestess can speak of wisdom given in dreams and visions.

Tarot and Spirit Communication

I believe that we always have spirits around us. We may see them as angels, guardians, deities, or those who have passed on. We may invoke them and ask for their guidance and protection, or they may choose to guide and watch over us.

People with the gift of mediumship can communicate with those spiritual entities. Channelers are able to let those entities speak through them.

Different people perceive Spirit in different ways. Part of the reason for that is cultural. Part of it is the different ways our gifts manifest. Some people see spirits, others hear them, others feel them.

Spirit can speak to us in our dreams or in our waking hours. Spirit can speak to us through tarot. Communication with Spirit can be as simple as pulling a card at random in answer to the question "What does the universe want me to know right now?" It can be as specific as "What is my deceased loved one doing right now?

If a querent has asked you to communicate with someone you didn't know in life, start by pulling cards to get a sense of who the person was in life. If there are issues related to the death, or if the death is recent or untimely, you can pull cards to describe how the individual experienced their own death. This is often helpful for the client, since the death experience usually reads as positive.

Often cards will come up to indicate other family members, also deceased, who now accompany the person in question.

You can ask direct questions of a spiritual entity, and interpret the cards pulled as your answer. You can pull cards to answer the questions "How can I communicate better with my guides and angels?" and "What do my guides and angels want me to know?"

You can leave specific cards on your altar as a message to those in Spirit or even as a request for assistance from them.

When asking "Which of my deceased loved ones is around me?" it is helpful to think about which cards represent which people. All tarot cards can indicate people. Some seem to do it more often than others. Of course, the Court cards, and certain Major Arcana cards, are often people. Try looking through your deck and deciding what sort of people might be indicated by other, less obvious, cards.

For instance, the Three of Pentacles could indicate a craftsperson. The Eight of Pentacles could indicate an apprentice. The Eight of Wands could indicate a runner. The Six of Wands could indicate a competitive person. The Ten of Pentacles could indicate an ancestor.

Sometimes the pictures of people in tarot cards look like someone you know. If I client says, "Oh, that looks just like my Aunt Mary!"—go with it. That's one of the ways Spirit speaks through tarot.

We can also use tarot to directly dialogue with our special spiritual guardians. Simply ask your guide to speak through the cards, ask your questions, and pull cards to receive the answers.

Specific cards can be used to invoke and communicate with specific saints, angels or deities. There are even tarot decks illustrated with Goddesses, angels, and saints. Using cards from those decks in invocation and communication can be particularly powerful.

Tarot as a Tool for Creative Visualization

Creative Visualization is a term that describes our ability to change our material world by changing the way we think. Many books have been written about this idea, from Edward Peach Ophiel's *The Art and Practice of Getting Material Things Through Creative Visualization* to the book by Shakti Gawain, entitled *Creative Visualization*, which was my first introduction to Creative Visualization. The same idea made its way to the bestseller list and to Oprah's couch with the 2006 film by Prime Time Productions called *The Secret*. From my study and experience, I believe that Creative Visualization is valid and effective. Here's how it works.

First, you need to set a clear goal for yourself. It can be a material possession, a new job, breaking a bad habit, weight loss, developing a skill or attracting a relationship.

Then, you need to picture yourself having already achieved that goal. Write about it in the present tense or draw a picture of it and think about it as if it is already happening. You need to be able to see yourself shopping for a size 8 dress, for instance, or driving your new BMW. You need to picture yourself sending out wedding invitations or going to work in your dream job. The more details you can think of, the more effective it will be.

Certain care needs to be taken here, along the lines of "be careful what you ask for, you may get it." Make sure that you really want what you think you want and try to think through any ripple-effect consequences that might be undesirable. It is also important to work on only one goal at a time, even if there is more than one change you would like to make in your life.

It is important that you set goals that are grounded in reality. At the same time, it is important to be able to imagine the best for yourself. Often the difference between successful people and frustrated people is simply that successful people believe in themselves and believe in their own success.

Meditation is an important tool in Creative Visualization. Once you have your goal set and are able to visualize it in the present tense, as if it were happening now, you should meditate with that vision. Breathe deeply and slowly and relax. Let all other thoughts leave your mind and focus only on your visualization. See it, and believe in it, and you will manifest it.

Tarot can make this process even easier and more effective. Each step of Creative Visualization is enhanced with the use of tarot.

Setting your goal can be the hardest part of this process. Perhaps you are not sure what you want. Perhaps you are not sure if what you want is realistic. Perhaps you want so many things you are not sure what to choose first.

If you are not sure what you want, shuffle the deck and pick one card at random to give you an idea of what sort of goal you should be setting.

If you have too many options, look through the deck and cognitively choose one card to represent each option. Shuffle just those cards and pick one of them at random to suggest your best choice.

If you have a goal, but are not clear on whether it is realistic, shuffle the whole deck, and think about your goal. Pick a card at random to let you know if this is an achievable goal at this time. The card you chose may also give you insight about obstacles or opportunities.

Once you have your goal set, shuffle the deck again. Now you want to ask if this is indeed a good thing to manifest. Pick a card, or a few cards, to give you an idea if this is a good thing to do, and if now is a good time to do it.

If your divination yields a positive result, shuffle your deck again. This time you will pull a card to ask if there is anything else you should do to strengthen your manifestation.

If your divination is negative, you might go back to the first step and pick another goal.

The next step is to create a solid visualization. You can do this with writing, drawing, collage, or simply imagining. However you choose to do it, why not strengthen it with tarot? Look through your tarot deck, and cognitively pick out cards that you feel represent your final goal, either through their images or meanings. Pick as many cards as you can find and arrange them in front of you. As you begin your meditative breathing, hold each card near your mouth, but far enough down that you can still see it. Actually breathe in the energy of the tarot card. Picture the energy of the card coming off the card and entering you through your breath. Leave the cards in front of you during your meditation. When you are finished, shuffle them back into your deck, confident of your positive outcome.

Once you have achieved your goal, make sure to have an attitude of gratitude!

Whenever you are ready, you can begin working on your next goal.

Through Creative Visualization, you can create healing, abundance, and success. With tarot as your guide, you can clearly choose the gifts that you most need at this time and manifest them quickly and effectively.

Tarot as a Map for the Spiritual Path

As we discussed in the very beginning of this book, tarot tells the story of a spiritual journey. It also can be used to set your own spiritual goals and mark the path to achieving them.

What are spiritual goals? They can be goals of self-improvement, or self-discovery. They can be goals of skill development. They can be goals of study or learning, or certification in a particular practice.

Some people would say that we all come into this life with specific goals for our spiritual development in this lifetime. Others would say that each person's goal is ultimately the same. Exactly what that goal is might be defined by one's spiritual or cultural background. It may be that, on a larger level, all goals are the same, whether we see it as achieving the perfection of Christ, experiencing enlightenment or solving the mystery.

In the Middle Ages there was great debate about the path to salvation. Some thought it came from knowledge and learning. Others thought it came from good deeds. Still others felt that accepting a religious doctrine was all that was needed.

In modern times, many of us don't think of the spiritual path in terms of salvation as much as we think of it in terms of finding enlightenment, integration, or personal peace.

It may be helpful to begin by simply asking the question "What did I come here to learn?" and pulling a card. "What do I want to learn while I am here?" is a substantially different but equally important question.

The Fool's journey through the Major Arcana teaches him responsibility, acceptance, and balance. He learns to cast off that which is no longer helpful, and thus experiences enlightenment. Arguably, we all make this same journey.

Divination with the Majors only may answer questions about the lessons you are working on currently. This process may be very helpful, since awareness of a lesson may lessen its severity.

You can create a tarot spread specific to your own spiritual journey and goals. You can do tarot magick to help you achieve these goals and to invoke spiritual guardians to help you along the way.

Here is the "Mapping the Spiritual Path" spread, performed May 7, 2011, for Sarah, as an example.

Figure 9 - Mapping the Spiritual Path for Sarah

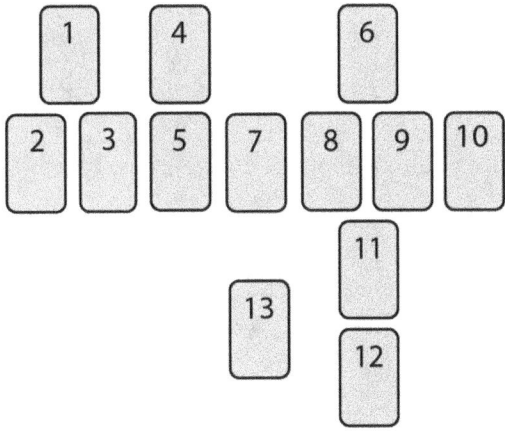

Card 1: What did I come here to learn?
    Sarah received the **Three of Cups**.
Card 2: How do those lessons manifest in my life?
    Sarah received the **World reversed**.
Card 3: What more must I do to learn those lessons?
    Sarah received the **Eight of Swords**.
Card 4: What do I want to learn?
    Sarah received the **Two of Cups reversed**.
Card 5: What must I do to learn this?
    Sarah received the **Hierophant reversed**.
Card 6: What is the ultimate goal of my spiritual path?
    Sarah received the **Three of Swords**.
Card 7: Actions to take supported by the element of Earth - Work and Stability
    Sarah received the **Seven of Pentacles**.
Card 8: Actions to take supported by the element of Air - Personal Integrity

*Sarah received the **Tower reversed**.*

Card 9: Actions to take supported by the element of Fire - Creativity and Growth

*Sarah received the **Six of Cups reversed**.*

Card 10: Actions to take supported by the element of Water - Emotions

*Sarah received the **Ace of Cups reversed**.*

Card 11: What tools do I have to help me along my path?

*Sarah received the **Lovers reversed**.*

Card 12: How do I unknowingly or unintentionally resist or sabotage my path?

*Sarah received the **Five of Cups**.*

Card 13: Where am I on my spiritual path right now?

*Sarah received the **Ace of Pentacles**.*

Sarah is a fifty-year-old small business owner. She is married with grown children. When I look at her spread overall, the first thing I notice is every Major Arcana card is reversed. The reversals do not necessarily indicate anything bad, but the trend should be noted. This suggests that Sarah has been choosing not to take as much of a spiritual focus in her life recently and/or that she has been nurturing attitudes that are counterproductive to her spiritual journey.

The next thing I notice is the two Three cards that show in similar positions. Card 1, "What did I come here to learn?" is the Three of Cups. Card 6, "What is the ultimate goal of my spiritual path?" is the Three of Swords. There is almost a bipolar energy here- the ability to swing between the positive and the negative. The Three of Swords can speak of healing for either one's self or others. The Three of Cups is a joyous card of community and frivolity.

A choice is rendered here: to choose healing, or to choose sorrow.

The two Pentacles cards stand out in the middle of the spread. They suggest groundedness. Sarah is best when she is working hard. Her business is part of her spiritual path, and her spirituality is connected to her appreciation of the Earth and nature.

As we look card-by-card, we start with the Three of Cups in the first position. What did Sarah come here to learn? She came here to learn to dance, sing, enjoy, have fun, and appreciate community. In short, Sarah came here to learn to celebrate life.

In the second position, the World reversed suggests that these lessons have not yet manifested in her life. In the third position, we see why. The Eight of Swords suggests that Sarah has an anxiety issue. She worries too much and traps herself. The stark difference between this card and the Three of Cups says it all.

Card 4, what she wants to learn, is the Two of Cups reversed. This could speak to wanting to understand love and all its complexities. Specific to this card are concepts of romantic love, self-love and self-esteem, and the healing nature of love.

In Card 5 we see that what she needs to do is find new ways of thinking and feeling, as represented by the Hierophant reversed. She needs to think outside of the box of her own anxieties. She may also need to learn new ways of understanding spirituality. The Hierophant reversed may suggest an exploration of alternative spirituality and new thought.

Since the Hierophant and the Two of Cups can suggest marriage, and they are both reversed, there may be a significant relationship problem for Sarah to consider.

Card 6 represents the ultimate goal of Sarah's spiritual path and is the Three of Swords. Especially in conjunction with the other cards, we clearly see the need for healing. It may be that Sarah has a calling to be a healer, or simply the need to heal herself.

The next four cards are elemental cards, and suggest what Sarah needs to do to further herself toward her goal. The Earth card is a Pentacles card, and the Water card is a Cups card (though reversed). It is particularly auspicious when the element of the card matches its position.

The Earth card is the Seven of Pentacles. Sarah needs to work hard and tend the garden that is her business and the garden of her spiritual growth.

The Air card is the Tower reversed. Sarah needs to heal from something that has changed her thought process. She may need to initiate another change in the way she thinks or in what she believes.

The Fire Card is the Six of Cups reversed. This is interesting because it is double the Three of Cups, so to speak. It seems that in the past, Sarah may have had more passion, more creativity, and more joy. Whatever has happened to her has changed that. Sarah needs to remember and reclaim her joy, her passion, and her creativity.

The Ace of Cups reversed in the Water position is nothing short of poignant. Once again, Sarah must heal her heart.

The most difficult card to interpret is the Lovers reversed in the eleventh position. What tools does Sarah have to help her? The Lovers would indicate she has the keen ability to make good decisions, to discern truth, to have a balanced relationship and to blend and integrate the many facets of her life. The problem is that the reversal would indicate that she is not using those tools effectively.

The twelfth card is obvious. How does Sarah hold herself back? The Five of Cups simply screams what we have already seen. Sarah is focusing on the negative rather than the positive. In that, she has been refusing to fulfill her greatest goal, to heal.

The final card is the Ace of Pentacles, describing where Sarah is right now. She is grounded in her work and in reality. She has a business to nurture and is connected to the Earth spiritually. The Ace indicates that she is just beginning her journey, but she has a good foundation from which to grow.

Stories from the Suit of Wands

As an adult female born under the sign of Scorpio, my Court card significator is the Queen of Cups. When I first started reading tarot professionally, I wasn't happy using the Queen of Cups to describe myself. As intuitive and expressive as that Queen can be, I felt Fire would be more helpful than Water in nurturing my new business.

My rising sign is Leo, a Fire sign. Whenever I did a reading for myself about my new business, the Queen of Wands figured prominently. It seemed that the Queen of Wands would show up to encourage me to market myself, to believe in myself, and to trust my intuition. Eventually, I adopted the Queen of Wands as my significator. To this day, she shows up in a reading to indicate that I am on the right track professionally, spiritually, and personally.

One day, just recently, I was having a bad day. I was short on patience and full of complaints. I was unkind to family members and untrusting of Spirit. That evening I had to teach a tarot class. The exercise was to pull one card at random to describe who we are at the present moment. The card I pulled was the Page of Wands. I explained to my class that I was normally the Queen of Wands. A new student piped up, laughing at me. "You've been demoted!" She said. And so I had. My immature behavior had registered in the cards, demoting me from Queen to Page.

Long before I ever thought of the sexual significance of tarot, or the phallic nature of the Wands, I was offering readings at a nightclub one Halloween. An extremely drunk man sat down with me and tried to hit on me. I had a long line waiting for readings and was in no mood for his sleazy shenanigans. I laid out the cards for him, and, wouldn't you know it, the Ace of Wands showed up as his significator. He interpreted it better than I did, though. He said to me "Hey, that looks like a big dick." No doubt.

Tarot Magick to Ignite the Fire Within

We all have times when we feel that we have lost our energy, our passion, our power or our "mojo." This can happen from boredom, heartbreak, overwork, or illness. This is a spell to use whenever you need to boost your energy, find your mojo, fuel your passions or find inspiration.

Pull from your tarot deck the Chariot, the Ace of Wands, the Four of Wands, the Eight of Wands and the Sun. I like to use many candles for this spell. If you use colored candles, Fire colors are best, like red, orange, and yellow. These are also the colors of the lower three chakras, which involve our sexuality, our wealth, our sense of security and our will.

Arrange your candles on your altar in whatever way seems right to you. Fresh flowers are helpful as well. If you burn incense, try myrrh, jasmine or sandalwood.

Start by breathing. Ground, center, and create sacred space. Drumming, dancing and chanting are good ways to create space and raise energy for this spell.

As you breathe, feel yourself grounded to the Earth, and bring energy into your lower three chakras. Move your legs and your hips to encourage the energy flow. Wiggle your toes, bend your knees and shake your hips.

When you are ready, take the Ace of Wands and hold it to your third chakra, the solar plexus, right below your ribcage. Breathe its energy into your solar plexus. As you do, say something like this:

"I bring Fire to my internal hearth. I fuel that Fire as I breathe. I stoke it as it burns within me, giving me the energy to dance, to create, to work and to inspire."

Then, take the Four of Wands and hold it to your heart, breathing its energy into the fourth chakra, your heart center. Say something like this:

"Passion, creativity, inspiration, joy, humor and motivation sustain me. May the fire energy within me sustain these things effortlessly, reliably and eternally."

Now take the Eight of Wands, the Chariot and the Sun, and hold then in a fan, in that sequence.

Carefully use the fan of cards to gently stir the candle flames, and incense smoke.

Here is a fun, rhyming incantation to finish your magickal work with Fire.

Say it as you stir the flames with your cards.

> "Dancing rising flames grow higher
>
> To excite, to heal and to inspire
>
> Inside me eternal Fire"

Leave the cards on your altar overnight. If possible, let your candles burn all the way out. Alternatively, you can burn them a little bit every day until they are gone.

May the element of Fire bless you on your journey.

A FINAL WORD

Continuing the Journey

Once aware of the four elements and their spiritual associations, it is easy to divide everything into your life into those four associations. This can be very helpful, as it gives you focus to nurture each facet of your life. It gives you a better ability to measure and maintain balance in your life.

Understanding the four elements is a fundamental way to understand your connection to all life around you, and to manifest the life you want.

When tarot enters your life, your life is improved. There are many roles tarot can play in your life. Do not feel you are any less able to enjoy tarot's benefits than any other tarot enthusiast is. It doesn't matter if you use it only for personal study, or if you are a collector of decks, a perpetual student, an artist, or a professional reader.

Your tarot journey can be a daily meditative practice. It can be a simple awareness of the elements and archetypes around you. It can be a path of healing for yourself and others. It can be a discipline of spiritual study. It can be a tool for creative and psychic development. It can be a business, or a ministry. The possibilities are endless. There is no need to make a decision regarding tarot in your future until you are ready. Set the goals that feel right for you and let your tarot journey unfold naturally. Each person's tarot journey is unique, just as each person's tarot reading style is unique.

Use tarot in the way that you enjoy it. Let it be a tour guide on your life's journey, as it brings you knowledge, fellowship, creativity, and a sense of connection to Spirit.

Bibliography and Recommended Reading

Over the past quarter-century, many books have contributed to my knowledge and practice of tarot. These are my favorites, and the ones that have been most helpful to me. Without the guidance of these authors, my own tarot career, and this book, would not have been possible.

Crowley, Aleister. *The Book of Thoth.* York Beach, ME: Weiser Books, 1974

Fairfield, Gail. *Every Day Tarot: A Choice Centered Book.* Boston MA: Red Wheel/Weiser LLC, 2002.

Giles, Cynthia. *The Tarot: History, Mystery and Lore.* New York, NY: Fireside, 1992.

Gray, Eden. *A Complete Guide to the Tarot.* New York, NY: Crown Publishers, Inc., 1970.

Greer, Mary K. *Tarot for Yourself: A Workbook for Personal Transformation.* North Hollywood, CA: Newcastle Publishing Co, Inc., 1984.

Katz, Marcus and Goodwin, Tali. *Secrets of the Waite-Smith Tarot.* Woodbury, MN: Llewellyn Publications, 2015

Kenner, Corrine. *Tarot for Writers.* Woodbury, MN: Llewellyn Publications, 2009.

Kraig, Donald Michael. *Tarot & Magic.* St. Paul MN: Llewellyn Publications, 2002.

Noble, Vicki and Jonathon Tenney. *Motherpeace Tarot Playbook: Astrology and the Motherpeace Cards.* Berkeley, CA: Wingbow Press, 1986.

Waite, Arthur Edward. *The Pictorial Key to the Tarot.* Stamford, CT: U.S. Games Systems, Inc., 2008

There are other books, not specifically related to tarot, that have also helped me on my spiritual journey. What I learned from them was equally essential in creating this book.

Gawain, Shakti. *Creative Visualization.* Berkeley, CA: Whatever Pub., 1978

Judith, Anodea. *Wheels of Life.* St. Paul, MN: Llewellyn Publications, 1990

Starhawk. *The Spiral Dance.* New York, NY: Harper Collins Publishers, 1988

Wolfe, Amber. *In the Shadow of the Shaman.* Woodbury, MN: Llewellyn Publications, 1988

Index of Figures and Tables

Figure 1 - Celtic Cross Spread 80
Figure 2 - Seven Sisters Spread 81
Figure 3 - Future Vision Spread 82
Figure 4 - The Lamplighter Spread 83
Figure 5 - Mapping the Spiritual Path Spread 84
Figure 6 - Compass Rose Spread 93
Figure 7 - Career Shifting Spread 141
Figure 8 - Looking for Love Card Dialogue 156
Figure 9 - Mapping the Spiritual Path for Sarah 191

Table 1 - Element of Fire Chart of Correspondences 88
Table 2 - Element of Earth Chart of Correspondences 89
Table 3 - Element of Air Chart of Correspondences 89
Table 4 - Element of Water Chart of Correspondences 90

About the Author

Christiana Gaudet has been a full-time professional tarot reader and teacher since 1993. She is the author of *Fortune Stellar: What Every Professional Tarot Reader Needs to Know.*

From her office in Palm City, Florida, she offers readings and instruction in person, and by telephone and internet.

www.christianagaudet.com

www.ingramcontent.com/pod-product-compliance
Lightning Source LLC
Chambersburg PA
CBHW052209090526
44584CB00016BA/1879